Volume 38   Number 2   2004

Discourse Processes

A MULTIDISCIPLINARY JOURNAL

Contents

Routledge
Taylor & Francis Group
New York   London

The Society for Text and Discourse Officers for 2004

President
Susan Goldman, *University of Illinois, Chicago*

Past President
Morton Ann Gernsbacher, *University of Wisconsin, Madison*

Secretary
Joe Magliano, *Northern Illinois University*

Treasurer
Max Louwerse, *University of Memphis*

Home Web Page
http://www.psyc.memphis.edu/ST&D/ST&D.htm

Editorial Office
Arthur Graesser
Department of Psychology
The University of Memphis
Campus Box 526400
Memphis, TN 38152–6400
E-mail: a-graesser@memphis.edu

Membership Offices

United States and Canada:
Max Louwerse
202 Psychology Building
Department of Psychology
The University of Memphis
Memphis, TN 38152–3230
E-mail: st-d@mail.psyc.memphis.edu

Outside United States and Canada:
Herre van Oostendorp
Institute of Information & Computing
Sciences
Utrecht Universit
3584 CS Utrecht, The Netherlands
E-mail: H.vanOostendorp@cs.uu.nl

First published by Lawrence Erlbaum Associates, Inc., Publishers
10 Industrial Avenue
Mahwah, New Jersey 07430

Reprinted 2009 by Routledge

Routledge

270 Madison Avenue
New York, NY 10016

2 Park Square, Milton Park
Abingdon, Oxon OX14 4RN, UK

ISBN 978-0-8058-9527-8

DISCOURSE PROCESSES, *38*(2), 169–172

INTRODUCTION

The Effects of Personal Involvement in Narrative Discourse

Max Louwerse
Department of Psychology/Institute for Intelligent Systems
University of Memphis

Don Kuiken
Department of Psychology
University of Alberta

Over the last several decades, the study of discourse processes has moved from the complementary efforts characteristic of multidisciplinary research to the explicitly integrative focus of interdisciplinary research (Graesser, Gernsbacher, & Goldman, 2003; Louwerse & Van Peer, 2002). Organizations like the International Society for the Empirical Study of Literature (IGEL), the International Association of Empirical Aesthetics, and the Poetics and Linguistics Association have supported the methodological and conceptual merger of areas such as literary studies, psychology, linguistics, and education. As is evident in this special issue, research concerning personal involvement in narrative discourse has benefitted from these developments.

Across disciplinary boundaries, a variety of terms have been used to identify personal involvement in narrative presentations. Readers may become *captured* by a literary text, moviegoers may become *entranced* by a cinematic narrative, members of an audience may be *moved* by a dramatic performance, and so on. Despite terminological diversity, something common seems at stake: Often during narrative encounters, feeling becomes fluid, comprehension seems multifaceted, and

---

Correspondence and requests for reprints should be sent to Don Kuiken, University of Alberta, Department of Psychology, P217 Biological Sciences Building, Edmonton, AB T6G 2E9 Canada. E-mail: dkuiken@ualberta.ca

the narrated world is brought vividly to presence. After such encounters, the presence of the narrative world often does not immediately dissipate. Lingering mood, changed beliefs, and shifts in self-perception indicate that something has not only been ingested, but also lastingly absorbed (Steiner, 1989, p. 9).

The research reported in this special issue indicates that there are, broadly considered, several sources of personal involvement:

- Personal involvement may be directly influenced by the setting, characters, and events that constitute the narrative world. Such involvement may be modulated by narrative structure (e.g., the narrative turns that provide suspense; Brewer & Lichtenstein, 1981) or specific narrative elements (e.g., the character morality that enables empathy; Zillman, 1994).
- Personal involvement may be affected when stylistic devices foster appreciation of the aesthetic quality of the narrative (Dixon, Bortolussi, Twilley, & Leung, 1993). Aesthetic appreciation may motivate continued or repeated consideration of the narrative (e.g., rereading a text).
- Personal involvement can be increased when stylistic devices (e.g., metaphors, alliteration) capture attention, unsettle conventional meanings, and evoke feeling (Miall & Kuiken, 1994; Van Peer, 1986). Personal involvement in this case initiates reinterpretive efforts that, because of their feeling connotations, are often self-implicating (Miall & Kuiken, 2002).

Often, these sources of personal involvement are conceived as though they depend on prior narrative comprehension. For example, imagery while reading may "fill in" what remains implicit in an explicitly presented narrative (Ingarden, 1973); empathy may supplement prior appraisal of concretely described character motives, attitudes, and beliefs (Zillman, 1994); and so on. In contrast, the studies in this special issue develop the possibility that personal involvement itself constitutes a primary mode of narrative comprehension. Thus, imagination may entail the projection of possibilities for understanding narrative events, empathy may involve the projection of possibilities for comprehending character development, and so on. Through such vivid and self-implicating projections, the import of the narrative is not only made manifest, but also absorbed into the reader's, viewer's, or listener's subsequent behavior.

The preceding conceptual reorientation reflects the influence of disciplines that traditionally emphasize the expressive aspects of narrative engagement. Not coincidentally, then, the authors contributing to this special issue represent social psychology, communication science, and literary studies. Their paths initially crossed in three separate but related settings. In 2002, a symposium at the conference of the IGEL in Pécs, Hungary, focused on "How Literature Enters Life." A workshop on the same theme in Cologne in 2002 and another in Utrecht in 2003 further concentrated interest in this issue. This confluence prompted us to invite five participants in these meetings to prepare their presentations for a journal that supports the inter-disciplinary character of the theme.

The benefits of personal involvement in narrative discourse are investigated by Eva-Wood. Her research tested a think-and-feel-aloud pedagogy on readers of po-etry in the classroom, comparing 11th-grade readers who focused on their personal responses with students who focused solely on textual analysis. Over the period of a month, students exposed to the think-and-feel-aloud pedagogy showed greater interest and engagement with poetry, participated more in classroom discussions, wrote significantly longer essays, and scored higher on comprehension tests than the textual-analysis group. Not only did this study find positive effects of personal involvement in narratives; it also demonstrated that these effects can be observed in younger readers, in reading poems, and in classroom settings.

Whereas Eva-Wood shows that verbalizing thoughts and feelings while reading poems plays a role in the involvement in narrative discourse, Hakemulder shows that textual features themselves can also cause this effect. He manipulates the pres-ence or absence of various stylistic devices (e.g., rhyme, inversion, metaphor, irony), often called *foregrounding*, that defamiliarize conventional conceptions of textual referents. Foregrounding increased reader appreciation of the text and prompted shifts in text-related social attitudes—but only among students in liter-ary studies and not among students from other disciplines (like sociology).

Beyond local stylistic variations, Konijn and Hoorn argue that *genre*, under-stood as the global features that establish narrative "realism," also increases per-sonal involvement. Although genre preference per se had little influence, the per-ceived realism of character representation had compelling effects on aesthetic appreciation and personal involvement.

Perceived realism also can be related to the reader's world knowledge of and ex-perience with the content of the narrative. Green reports that readers who thought that a narrative was realistic became more involved in that story. The extent to which readers thought that characters acted like real people was influenced by the reader's prior knowledge and social experience, suggesting facilitated identifica-tion with familiar characters.

The role of personal identification of the reader with the story character was also investigated by Kuiken et al. They found that readers who repeatedly linked the narrative to their own personal experiences by using story characters as meta-phoric vehicles in self-referential statements were more likely to report reading-in-duced shifts in self-perception. Readers who reflected on the story in this way were also more likely to score high in a personality measure of openness to experience.

The five studies reported in this special issue examine a range of potential deter-minants of personal involvement in narrative discourse. These include overt ver-balization of thoughts and feelings (Eva-Wood), foregrounding (Hakemulder), preference for genre and protagonists (Konijn & Hoorn), relevance of the content of a text to the reader (Green), and identifying with a character (Kuiken et al.).

These studies also examine different aspects of what is absorbed by the reader, including sophisticated forms of questioning (Eva-Wood), lasting appreciation of story points (Hakemulder), involvement with story characters (Konijn & Hoorn), commitment to story-consistent beliefs (Green), and changes in the sense of self (Kuiken et al.). Collectively, these studies challenge our conception of what it means to understand media presentations of fictional narratives as well as our conception of the strategies through which such understanding is attained.

ACKNOWLEDGMENTS

We would like to thank reviewers for their help in this special issue. The workshop "How Literature Enters Life" in Cologne in 2002 was supported by the German Science Association (DFG). The workshop with the same title, held in Utrecht in 2003, was supported by the Dutch Science Organization (NWO), the Utrecht Research Institute for History and Culture (OGC), and the Dutch Graduate School for Literary Studies (OSL).

REFERENCES

Brewer, W. F., & Lichtenstein, E. H. (1981). Event schemas, story schemas, and story grammars. In J. Long & A. Baddeley (Eds.), *Attention and performance* (Vol IX, pp. 363–379). Hillsdale, NJ: Lawrence Erlbaum Associates, Inc.

Dixon, P., Bortolussi, M., Twilley, L. C., & Leung, A. (1993). Literary processing and interpretation: Toward empirical foundations. *Poetics, 22,* 5–33.

Graesser, A. C., Gernsbacher, M. A., & Goldman, S. (Eds.). (2003). *Handbook of discourse processes.* Mahwah, NJ: Lawrence Erlbaum Associates, Inc.

Ingarden, R. (1973). *The cognition of the literary work of art* (R. A. Crowley & K. R. Olson, Trans.). Evanston, IL: Northwestern University Press. (Original work published 1931)

Louwerse, M. M., & Van Peer, W. (2002). *Thematics: Interdisciplinary studies.* Amsterdam: Benjamins.

Miall, D. S., & Kuiken, D. (1994). Foregrounding, defamiliarization, and affect: Response to literary stories. *Poetics, 22,* 389–407.

Miall, D. S., & Kuiken, D. (2002). A feeling for fiction: Becoming what we behold. *Poetics, 30,* 221–241.

Steiner, G. (1989). *Real presences.* Chicago: University of Chicago Press.

Van Peer, W. (1986). *Stylistics and psychology: Investigations of foregrounding.* London: Croom Helm.

Zillman, D. (1994). Mechanisms of emotional involvement with drama. *Poetics, 23,* 33–51.

DISCOURSE PROCESSES, *38*(2), 173–192

How Think-and-Feel-Aloud Instruction Influences Poetry Readers

Amy L. Eva-Wood

Teacher Education Program
University of Washington, Seattle

Assuming readers' emotional responses can inform literary analysis, this study of poetry readers featured an instructional intervention that involved modeling both cognitive and affective reading processes through a think-and-feel-aloud pedagogy. Eleventh-grade students in 2 conditions participated in a 4-week unit on reading poetry. Control group instruction focused on textual analysis and vocabulary building, whereas experimental group instruction focused on readers' personal responses, which were mapped back to textual elements. Experimental group students reported more favorable orientations to poetry and wrote longer responses to poems than control group students. Analysis of classroom discourse revealed that the experimental group participated in discussions more frequently and asked more sophisticated text-based questions while identifying with the poem's speakers.

When readers claim to resonate with a striking literary passage, what really happens? A poignant phrase can illuminate a reader's understanding as it gives voice to previously unarticulated thoughts or feelings. Readers who actively engage poetic language can be sensitized to the textures and flavors of life experiences that might have otherwise remained inexplicable. The 2001–2002 U.S. poet laureate Billy Collins (2001) claimed that the study of poetry provides a model for learning:

> I came to realize that to study poetry was to replicate the way we learn and think. When we read a poem, we enter the consciousness of another. It requires that we loosen some of our fixed notions in order to accommodate another point of view— which is a model of the kind of intellectual openness and conceptual sympathy that a liberal education seeks to encourage. (p. B5)

Correspondence and requests for reprints should be sent to Amy L. Eva-Wood, University of Washington, Teacher Education Program, Box 353600, 211 Miller Hall, Seattle, WA 98195. E-mail: aevawood@u.washington.edu.

Thus, poetry can offer its readers opportunities to stretch their awareness, adapt their perspectives, and construct new knowledge in a way that many expository texts cannot.

Yet student readers, bogged down in the mechanics of poetry, may not be capable of this level of engagement with poetic language (Earthman, 1992; Harker, 1994). When they focus all of their energies on decoding literary devices and charting rhyme schemes, poetry does not hold the same power to personally challenge and impress. Students of poetry learn to remove themselves objectively from a text to analyze its technical structure. Words, in this case, become cumbersome, unwieldy, and menacing. Unfortunately, the rules of this analytical undertaking can deter students from openly engaging with language, responding to its nuances, and expanding their perspectives.

Language arts educators face the ongoing dilemma that occurs in the troublesome negotiation between the mechanics of reading and the experience of reading. Yet literary analysis can coexist and even complement personal, experiential responses to poetry. Rosenblatt (1995) suggested that literature provides students with the opportunity "to think rationally within an emotionally colored context" (p. 217). Literary texts can serve as bases for the dynamic interplay between affective and cognitive processes. How would readers react if they were not only given permission, but also prompted to draw on their personal responses while "making sense" of poetry? If they relied more deliberately on affect to scout out poetic territory, would they find themselves more inclined to engage the cognitive demands of the process?

To supplement cognitive models of text processing (e.g., Gernsbacher, 1990; Kintsch, 1988, 1998; van den Broek, Young, Tzeng, & Linderholm, 1999; Zwaan, Langston, & Graesser, 1995), literary response researchers argue for a theoretical model that acknowledges the role of affect in readers' understanding of literary texts. Although few studies examine readers' emotional responses to literary texts, they tend to center around short stories rather than poetry. However, several think-aloud studies with poetry (Earthman, 1992; Harker, 1994; Peskin, 1998) indicate that readers might benefit from a more open, active, and multifaceted approach to reading.

STUDENTS' READING STRUGGLES: WHAT THINK-ALOUD RESEARCH REVEALS

In a think-aloud study with high school readers, Harker (1994) found that many read poetry as if it were prose, requiring "plain sense" (p. 212) translation.[1] In an analysis of expert and novice think-aloud protocols, Peskin (1998) discovered that

---

[1]Richards (1929) defined poetry's "plain sense" as "its prose sense, its plain, overt meaning, as a set of ordinary intelligible English sentences, taken quite apart from any further poetic significance" (p. 12).

college freshmen actually did have a basic understanding of poetry as a discourse; however, they did not know what to do with that discourse knowledge and used very few interpretative strategies when contrasted with expert readers. Similarly, Earthman's (1992) findings revealed that novice readings of literature tended to be "closed," whereas experts read in a more "open" manner. College freshmen demonstrated quick and simple one-dimensional interpretations, whereas graduate students displayed more comfort with ambiguity and a willingness to accommodate various levels of meaning. If novices, like more experienced readers, could better sense and appreciate the rich connotative nature of words and language, they might be less intimidated when befuddled by a poem and might value the meaning-making process as an open, exploratory experience with words.

Wineburg (1991) drew from Roland Barthes (1974) to illuminate the differences between experts and novices who read historical texts. Barthes contrasted "readerly" texts with "writerly" texts (p. 503). Readerly texts convey straightforward messages, whereas writerly texts challenge conventions. By talking with their texts, readers learn to engage personally to decipher the author's voice and context and ultimately construct meaning. This process of explicating a writerly text parallels some of the strategies utilized in literary analysis, where literary critics also assume that texts are writerly—not simple, straightforward, and readerly, as some student readers demonstrate in their "plain sense" and "closed" poetry analyses (Earthman, 1992; Harker, 1994).

EXPANDING TEXT PROCESSING THEORIES
TO ACCOMMODATE EMOTIONAL RESPONSE

Text processing theories have often focused on cognitive processes generalized to all text types. Recently, a shift has taken place. For instance, Kintsch (1998) addressed comprehension processes that are particular to literary texts. Although claiming that literary readers process texts in the fashion of his Construction Integration model (Kintsch, 1988), he stressed that the surface features of literary texts powerfully influence a reader's memory and comprehension. Although Kintsch (1998) did not fully develop a theory of literary processing, he attempted to speak to the concerns of Miall and Kuiken (1994), who argued that text comprehension models focusing purely on propositional, inferential, and elaborative processes cannot necessarily be applied to literary texts and their unique use of stylistic devices.

To address literary processing more directly, Miall and Kuiken (1994) discussed *defamiliarization,* a process that readers undergo in response to stylistic devices (e.g., metaphors, similes, and grammatical or phonemic deviations) particular to literary texts (e.g., poems, short stories). It involves a departure from prototypical understandings of words and relations between words—a departure from normal language—and evokes feelings, personal perspectives, and personal meanings[2] (see also Hoffstaedter, 1987).

If readers tend to respond to literary devices with feelings, personal perspectives, and personal meanings as Miall and Kuiken (1994) suggested, then potentially confused novice readers might benefit from instruction that pays special attention to these personal responses. For example, Feagin (1996) proposed that readers should examine their emotional responses to literature by asking themselves, "What warrants this reaction?" In posing such a question, they may be able to track their responses back to specific words or images. Readers' careful monitoring of their emotional responses, therefore, could be the key to unlocking meanings in poems and other literary works. Thus, an instructional focus on feelings and personal responses might help students bypass the initial cognitive pressure to determine "the meaning" in a poem.

BROADENING NOTIONS
OF COGNITIVE APPRENTICESHIP

The literature on "cognitive apprenticeship" (A. Collins, Brown, & Newman, 1989), although it does not explicitly account for emotional response, provides a foundation for the development of such instruction. The *cognitive apprenticeship metaphor* suggests a pedagogical method that makes inherently invisible and abstract thinking skills palpable and observable for the learner. Surprisingly, the cognitive apprenticeship literature does not clearly and explicitly feature the practice of *thinking aloud*—verbalizing all of one's uncensored thoughts while working through a problem such as reading an unfamiliar text. Yet the relation between cognitive apprenticeship and thinking aloud seems straightforward and fairly seamless. Genuine instructional modeling can take place when teachers extemporaneously share their reading strategies and struggles with their students while working their way through a literary passage.

CREATING A THINK-AND-FEEL-ALOUD PEDAGOGY

The general text processing theories mentioned earlier and the apprenticeship literature focus primarily on cognitive issues without acknowledging affective processes, which can also play a vital role in student learning, particularly in litera-

---

[2]Miall and Kuiken (1994) acknowledged that their defamiliarization theory builds on the principles of early 19th-century Romantic theorists (Coleridge, 1817/1983) in addition to the theories of the Russian Formalist group (Shklovsky, 1917/1965) and the Prague Linguistic Circle (Mukarovsky, 1932/1964) in the early 20th century.

ture-based learning. One of the problems students face when reading poems is that they focus too much on "making sense" of the poem, even though some of the defamiliarizing stylistic devices may be serving to counter that effort. If emotions can play a role in helping readers understand stylistic devices and interpret poems, then more explicit discussion of emotional response in literature classrooms should be emphasized. Furthermore, if modeling serves as the key function of cognitive apprenticeship, the most direct form of modeling in a poetry classroom would most likely be captured within the context of the think-and-feel-aloud process, which requires teachers and student readers to voice all of their thoughts and feelings as they read a poem aloud.

Therefore, this study incorporated a richer, fuller, more complete cognitive apprenticeship pedagogy that featured modeling through the think-and-feel-aloud process. The study design addressed the benefits of an instructional intervention, which featured explicit modeling and discussion of both cognitive and affective responses to poems. Based on the influence of the designed intervention, I hypothesized that (a) students might report greater interest and engagement with the reading process and (b) both their written work and classroom discussions might also reflect a higher level of engagement in analysis and more sophisticated responses to the poems addressed.

METHOD

Forty students from two 11th-grade classrooms participated in a 4-week unit on reading and responding to poetry. The control group ($n = 21$), collaboratively taught by an award-winning classroom English teacher and myself, received regular instruction in literary analysis, as planned by their teacher. The experimental group ($n = 19$), also collaboratively taught, received instruction designed to highlight emotional and experiential facets of poetry reading, building on the pedagogical methods of "cognitive apprenticeship" proposed by A. Collins et al. (1989). Both the classroom teacher and myself were aware of the two conditions; therefore, we taught both groups together to counter possible teacher effects and to work together to match instruction between the groups as much as possible. For example, students in both groups generally received the same proportion of instructional and discussion time despite differing pedagogical approaches. In addition, both teachers tended to step back as research-facilitators and observe the large-group discussions that served as data for this study.

Participants

The participant sample ($n = 40$) was drawn from two of the collaborating teacher's American literature classrooms at a suburban high school in the northwest United

TABLE 1
Establishing Group Equivalence

Verbal Intelligence Measures	N	M	SD
English grade			
Control	21	83.84	8.88
Intervention	19	85.57	8.53
Listening score			
Control	18	456.28	49.92
Intervention	18	470.17	54.84
Reading score			
Control	18	409.28	16.78
Intervention	18	413.50	17.73
Writing score			
Control	18	9.11	1.23
Intervention	18	8.83	1.79

States. The study featured 11th graders—based on the assumption that they had basic familiarity with poetry and would be able to engage fairly complex poems. Group means for the students' English semester grades and state assessment scores in listening, reading, and writing served as imperfect proxies for equating the two groups on verbal intelligence. Group mean scores were not different ($p > .19$ in all cases) and therefore allowed for analyses based on the assumption of group equivalence (see Table 1).

Study Design

Students in both the control and experimental groups participated in a 4-week unit on reading poetry, which featured works by American poets Emily Dickinson, Robert Frost, e.e. cummings, and Langston Hughes. Students began the unit by reviewing literary terms on a "Poetry Basics" handout. After taking a quiz on literary terms (i.e., *alliteration, simile, metaphor, stanza, rhyme scheme*, etc.), both groups participated in a "Museum Style Poetry" activity where they selected poetic language that appealed to them and posted it on the classroom walls the following week. Students roamed the class, read, and enjoyed each other's selections. Other common activities throughout the unit included freewriting in response to poems, visualizing and drawing images or scenes from poems, and participating in informal game-show-style quizzes on materials read. To complete the unit, both groups also turned in a culminating project featuring research on a famous musician with a critique of the musician's lyrics.

Despite these common elements, the instructors' pedagogical goals and strategies differed significantly in the two classrooms (see Table 2). Control group instruction generally featured literary analysis and vocabulary building. The control

TABLE 2
Instructional Orientations for Control and Intervention Groups

Group	Control	Intervention
Group process	Small group discussions Literary analysis in pairs Large group discussions	Teacher think and feel alouds Think and feel alouds in pairs Large group discussions
Teachers' roles	Discussion leader/facilitator	Discussion leader/facilitator Think-aloud model/coach
Orientation to poetry	Emphasis on vocabulary building and line-by-line interpretation of poem	Emphasis on initial experience of poem and mapping this response back to a poem's textual elements
Curricular emphasis	Literary analysis	Reader response (using think and feel alouds)
Guiding questions	What do you think this poem is about? What does this mean?	What do you see and feel? What strikes you as you read?

classroom received instruction that focused more on the technical aspects of poetry reading. During classroom discussions, they read poems both silently and aloud, discussed unfamiliar vocabulary and literary terms, and commented on the poem's possible meanings in large and small groups.

Experimental group instruction focused on reader response as a precursor to discussing textual elements. After teachers shared and modeled their personal responses, students learned to verbalize their own thoughts and feelings aloud, in a stream-of-consciousness fashion, while they read poems. Students practiced this form of response in pairs; as one student read and commented aloud, the other student noted the reader's responses. Then the pair analyzed their notes together, identifying each other's salient emotions, the specific words and phrases analyzed, and the interpretive questions and comments made. As students participated in several think-and-feel-aloud activities, they began to develop a working list of interpretive strategies as a class.

The instructors' roles also varied slightly from control to experimental group. In the control classroom, the instructors primarily served as discussion leaders and facilitators, whereas in the experimental classroom, instructors were not only facilitators, but initially served as models when they verbalized their thoughts and feelings while reading poems aloud. Guiding questions for discussions also ranged. During control group discussions, questions revolved around word meanings, literary terms, and themes. In the experimental group, however, guiding questions prompted students to discuss their experience of the poems. What did they see or feel? What surprised or caught them off guard? Instructors helped experimental group students to link their experience of the poem back to literary elements.

Group Measures

Students in both the control and experimental classrooms completed three measures before and after participating in the instructional unit: (a) an informal essay response to a poem; (b) a short-answer response to the same poem; and (c) a poetic response questionnaire, which assessed students' attitudes and approaches to reading poetry. On completion of the written response portion of the assessment, students received the short-answer question and then the poetic response questionnaire. All students comfortably finished the three measures within the 1-hr time limit set for completion.

Written responses. Two equivalent forms, each addressing a different poem, were counterbalanced and given as a pre- and postunit assessment to both the control and experimental groups. Students read the instructions: "Read and respond to this poem. What do you think this poem is about? What are its possible meanings?" Then, they wrote a brief response to the poem. The two poems selected for the pre- and postunit assessment were sonnets written by the American poet, May Sarton. Both poems have identical structures and a central metaphor. The first poem, Sonnet 6 from "These Images Remain," revolves around the metaphor of sculpting to depict the creative process, whereas the second poem, Sonnet 2 from "The Autumn Sonnets," centers on themes of loss through the metaphor of falling leaves.

Researchers scored students' written responses based on Wallace-Jones's (1991) 4-level scale designed specifically to evaluate adolescents' cognitive responses to poetry. Students received a score of 1 for a *low-level generalization* about the poem or a response based on a single word or phrase. Scores increased as they integrated numerous references from the poem to examine its possible meanings. Students were awarded the highest score of 4 when attention to detail was coupled with a larger exploration of the poem's metaphors. In these responses, students' references were supported by knowledge of the world as they began to integrate "overview and detail." Evaluating 20% of the data, three researchers who were unaware of the two conditions achieved 92% reliability.

To supplement pre- and postunit essays, students answered an additional short-answer question with responses of only one or two sentences. This similarly worded question also tapped students' understanding of the poems' possible meanings, asking for a more succinct version of their essay responses. One-point responses featured a brief, surface-level statement of topic, which may have been drawn directly from the text. Students received 2 points for a brief, yet plausible elaboration on the poem's meanings (beyond a literal restatement of the poem's topic or content). Finally, students received 3 points when they responded with a plausible interpretation developed with two or more complete thoughts and possible textual references. Three independent scorers, unaware of the two conditions, evaluated the short-answer responses and achieved 96% reliability after scoring 20% of the data.

Poetic response questionnaire.   A pre- and postunit assessment of students' attitudes and beliefs about poetry complemented the analysis of their written responses. Students completed the poetic response questionnaire by reading each of the 18 statements (e.g., "Poetry makes me sensitive to aspects of my life that I usually ignore" or "I can easily visualize images described in a poem") and rating their level of agreement with each statement on a 4-point Likert scale ranging from 1 (*strongly disagree*) to 4 (*strongly agree*).

The items in this brief survey were taken from Miall and Kuiken's (1995) Literary Response Questionnaire (LRQ) and adapted slightly to address poetry rather than stories and novels. Only those items were included for which Miall and Kuiken reported the highest factor loadings (ranging from .51 to .84) for six of seven factors.[3] These factors, which addressed readers' orientations to literature, included the following: insight, empathy, imagery vividness, leisure escape, concern with author, and rejection of literary values. All scales in the LRQ retained "satisfactory internal consistency, retest reliability, and factorial validity" (Miall & Kuiken, 1995, p. 37). In this study, internal consistency measures for both the adapted questionnaire as a whole and its subscales at posttest are represented by the following alpha coefficients: insight (.77), empathy (.67), imagery vividness (.75), leisure escape (.80), concern with author (.68), and rejection of literary values (.78, reverse scored for the aggregated scale), and the poetic response total score (.80).

Statistical Analysis

I evaluated intervention effects with a one-way analysis of covariance (ANCOVA) in which pretest scores were used as covariates in the assessment of differences between posttest scores. This statistical design was applied to scores on all group measures (i.e., informal essay responses, short-answer responses, and poetic response questionnaires). Although I had established group equivalence based on English grades and standardized test scores, this design took into account possible group differences on the study's pretests and attempted to equalize groups even further by adjusting for these differences.

---

[3]I excluded items representing one of the seven factors (i.e., "story-driven reading") in the LRQ (Miall & Kuiken, 1995) because these items focused exclusively on narratives (rather than poetry).

Discourse Analysis

Acknowledging reading as a "socially embedded activity" (Pressley & Afflerbach, 1995), I audiotaped and analyzed whole group and small group conversations in both classrooms as students and teachers discussed several poems. Three similarly structured classroom discussions were selected for analysis. Two discussions took place midway through the instructional unit, and the third discussion occurred on the final day of instruction. I analyzed classroom discourse in the control and experimental conditions based on the following: (a) student participation: Who spoke? How often? (b) text-based questions: How many questions did students ask about the poems? What types of questions did students ask? and (c) identification with the poems' speakers: Did students identify with the speakers in some of the poems? If so, in what ways? To frame my analysis, I drew primarily on Nystrand's (1997) research, which examined the advantages of dialogically organized approaches to learning in language arts classrooms. Open coding procedures (Strauss, 1987) focused on the types of comments students made as they interacted with teachers, texts, and peers.

RESULTS

Poetic Response Questionnaire: Students' Engagement With Poetry

Students completed the poetic response questionnaire by reading each of the 18 statements and rating their level of agreement with each statement. An ANCOVA revealed significant differences between the control and experimental group's interest and engagement with poetry, $F(1, 35) = 9.12$, $MSE = .09$, $p < .01$. The control group's adjusted mean score ($M = 2.60$, $SE = .07$) was significantly lower than the experimental group's adjusted mean ($M = 2.89$, $SE = .07$) at the posttest.

In addition, significant differences between means emerged in two of the six component subscales. First, the control group's adjusted mean score ($M = 2.18$, $SE = .11$) on the reading as leisure escape subscale was significantly lower than the experimental group's adjusted mean ($M = 2.52$, $SE = .11$) at the posttest, $F(1, 35) = 4.46$, $MSE = .22$, $p < .05$. Second, the control group's adjusted mean score ($M = 2.15$, $SE = .13$) for the concern with author subscale was also significantly lower than the experimental group's adjusted mean ($M = 2.60$, $SE = .13$) at the posttest, $F(1, 35) = 5.49$, $MSE = .35$, $p < .05$. Adjusted mean differences at posttest approached significance for both the insight and empathy subscales ($p = .06$ and $p = .07$, respectively). However, mean differences for the last two subscales, imagery vividness and rejection of literary values, were not significant.

TABLE 3
Adjusted Group Means for Students' Written Responses

Written Response Measures	Control[a]		Intervention[b]	
	M	SE	M	SE
Informal essay (number of words)[c]	83.88	9.61	123.24	9.89
Informal essay (holistic response score)[d]	1.99	0.13	2.13	0.13
Short answer question (response score)[e]	1.53	0.19	2.22	0.20

[a]$n = 19$. [b]$n = 18$. [c]Pretest covariate = 90.11. [d]Pretest covariate = 2.03. [e]Pretest covariate = 1.97.

Students' Written Responses: Exploring Possible Meanings in Poems

In addition, students in both groups read an unfamiliar poem before and after participating in the instructional unit. Then, they responded to the following prompt in an informal, freewritten essay: "What do you think this poem is about? What are its possible meanings?" Furthermore, students completed a short-answer question to supplement their informal essay responses to a poem. The question prompted a more concise version (one or two sentences in length) of the students' essay response. Table 3 presents the adjusted means for students' written responses. The means represent (a) the average number of essay words written and (b) the average holistic response score students received for their essay, based on the Wallace-Jones (1991) 4-level scale. The final row features the short-answer score group means based on a 1 through 3 scale.

Students in the experimental group wrote significantly longer essays than control group students, $F(1, 34) = 8.0$, $MSE = 1722.57$, $p < .01$, whereas group differences on holistic response scores were not significant ($F < 1$). However, the experimental group students scored significantly higher than the control group on their short-answer responses, $F(1, 34) = 4.19$, $MSE = .70$, $p < .05$.

Classroom Discourse

To complement the information that pre- and posttests provided, qualitative analyses of similarly structured classroom discussions indicated differences in (a) students' voluntary participation, (b) the quality of questions students asked, and (c) their personal identification with the poems' speakers.

Participation. Based on the sample of three discussions scheduled during the second half of the instructional unit, students in the experimental classroom participated in the large group discussions more frequently than students in the control classroom. On average, 12 experimental group students participated in each classroom discussion, making over 34 comments per session, whereas an average of only 6 students participated in each control group discussion, making 17 comments per session.

Students' questions.   Student-initiated questions asked during the final discussion of the unit differed in their level of sophistication and fell into three categories based on open coding (Strauss, 1987). These included (a) procedural, (b) understanding, and (c) interpreting questions. Lower level procedural questions generally involved asking for repetition or clarification regarding a previous speaker's comments, or they related to classroom instructions and activities (e.g., "What are we supposed to do?" or "Where?"); however, procedural questions did not relate directly to textual material. Questions of understanding were essentially simple questions of meaning, which related to words or phrases that students did not recognize or comprehend (e.g., "What does this word mean?" and "What does it mean when the speaker says … ?"). Interpreting questions were text based—fundamental to further analysis of the poem discussed. These higher level questions fell into three subcategories: (a) philosophical questions (e.g., "Can't you love after you're dead?"); (b) questions regarding themes and larger meanings (e.g., "Is [the speaker] mad at God?"); and (c) speculative questions, which included a brief, tentative interpretation in response to a line or phrase in the text (e.g., "'Prevent the dog from barking with a juicy bone.' No more fun [for the poem's speaker]?").

Control group students asked lower level procedural (50%) and understanding (50%) questions during the discussion without advancing to higher level interpreting questions. In contrast, only a small proportion (20%) of the experimental group's questions was procedural, whereas the majority were understanding (40%) and interpretive (40%) questions. In this case, the experimental group's questions indicated a greater level of engagement with the text and a more sophisticated analytical orientation.

Identification with a poem's speaker.   Aside from the questions asked, students in the experimental group revealed greater personal engagement with the poem's speaker. Analysis of the three class discussions revealed that experimental classroom students commented more frequently (31 times) about the speaker's thoughts and feelings than the control classroom students (12 comments). For example, students elaborated on one poem by relating to the speaker's loss of a loved one. One student in the experimental group claimed, "I think she just wants life to stop for her and the world to stop. Because when someone leaves you … you want everything to just stop. You just want time to stop." Several other students in the experimental group elaborated similarly (e.g., "You don't really want to do anything because time's just standing" and "You know after you lose somebody, you don't want to see anything, you want to just stay in your room and pout").

These examples illustrate another noteworthy trend in the data. Students' use of pronouns indicated further evidence of their identification with the speakers in the poems. Experimental group students frequently used the second-person pronoun (*you*) in reference to the poems' speakers (12 times), whereas control group students generally used third-person pronouns (e.g., *he* or *she*) to refer to the poems' speakers (using *you* only twice over all three discussions). The use of a collective *you* obscures the referent—is it the student, the poem's speaker, or perhaps those individuals in the classroom and beyond? Some linguists (e.g., Harley & Ritter, 2002) have argued that second-person inclusive pronouns are closer to first-person forms. This distinctive use of pronouns suggests that experimental group students identified with the poems' speakers while perhaps framing their experiences as commonly shared.

DISCUSSION

The purpose of this study was to examine the potential benefits of a think-and-feel-aloud pedagogy on poetry readers. Combining the theories of Miall and Kuiken (1994) and Feagin (1996), which point to the informing role of a reader's emotional responses, I developed an instructional intervention that enlarged traditional notions of cognitive apprenticeship (A. Collins et al., 1989). This form of instruction, which featured the explicit modeling of both cognitive and affective processes, influenced the experimental group in several ways.

First, based on an adapted version of Miall and Kuiken's (1995) LRQ, the experimental groups' posttest scores reflected greater interest and engagement with poetry when compared with the control group. Second, students in the experimental group wrote significantly longer posttest essays than control group students, suggesting a greater comfort level with literary analysis and more personal investment in the writing process. Third, experimental group students scored significantly higher than control group students in their posttest short-answer responses to a poem, demonstrating their ability to comment thoughtfully on a poem's possible meanings. Finally, experimental group students participated in classroom discussions more frequently; identified with the poems' speakers; and asked more sophisticated, text-based questions than their control group counterparts. These results suggest that there may be merit in utilizing a think-and-feel-aloud pedagogy, which prompts student readers to identify their affective responses and relate them back to textual elements.

The study's theoretical framework draws from Miall and Kuiken's (1994) *defamiliarization theory*, which emphasizes the primary role of stylistic elements in influencing readers' emotions and personal responses. However, results also provide evidence to substantiate the equally important role of "narrative feelings" (Miall & Kuiken, 2002) or "fiction emotions" (Kneepkens & Zwaan, 1994) in driving poetry readers' interpretations. Many readers in this study readily identified with speakers (and characters) in the poems they read. In addition, these affective responses—taking the form of sympathy for or empathy with the speakers' experiences—may have served to temper the confusion some students felt when confronted with defamiliarizing textual elements. In his research, Goetz (1996) "found that emotional response ... is constructive, in that most of the terms readers used to describe their emotional responses did not appear in the [text]" (p. 235). The affective responses featured in the classroom discourse data tended to help students actively develop their interpretations and elaborate more openly (Earthman, 1992) on the poems they discussed.

Personal Engagement With Poetry

As a self-report measure, the poetic response questionnaire does not indicate the level of sophistication with which students analyze a poem. However, it does serve as a useful tool because it suggests positive changes in readers' motivations for reading, their reading priorities, and their level of engagement with poetry. Furthermore, accounting for the length of students' essays does not address the quality of thought in their written work, but it can suggest a certain comfort level with a writing task. In addition, a greater number of words written might indicate a more positive orientation toward poetry and a stronger personal response to a poem. If this outcome reflects increased interest and investment in literary analysis, then it complements the experimental group's self-report data from the poetic response questionnaire.

Likewise, in three similarly structured discussions, experimental group students participated in classroom discussions more than control group students did. On average, experimental group students made twice as many unsolicited comments as control group students. Student self-selection of this nature is a feature of dialogically organized instruction, which promotes learning (Gutierrez, 1993). "Compared with recitation, dialogic instruction involves fewer teacher questions and more conversational turns as teachers and students alike contribute their ideas to a discussion in which their understandings evolve" (Nystrand, 1997, p. 17).

Experimental group students' comments often focused on the poems' speakers, providing further evidence of their personal engagement with the poems discussed in class. Students frequently speculated about the speakers' thoughts and feelings, often using second-person pronouns (*you*), which suggests identification with the speakers' experiences. Dadlez (1997) stated, "Empathetic responses to literature can often provide the clearest route to a work's ethical perspective on the human condition or on human nature, for empathy involves imaginatively entering into a perspective other than one's own" (p. 191). Students in the experimental group who related to the speakers' experiences may have been more likely to sense the poems' larger themes and implications.

Textual Analysis

Students in the experimental group asked higher level, text-based questions (i.e., interpreting questions) when compared with students in the control group who only asked procedural questions (revolving around classroom activities) and basic questions of understanding. This suggests that students in the control group may not have been as invested in the poems they read and discussed. Heath (1978) distinguished procedural display from substantive engagement. If control group students are simply going through the motions of school, as indicated by their procedural questions, they are less likely to learn from the poems they discuss. However, the experimental group's text-based, interpretive questions reflect critical thinking and a more sophisticated approach to literary analysis.

However, this distinction between groups was not reflected in their informal essay scores. Based on the Wallace-Jones (1991) scale, differences between groups on posttest holistic response scores were not significant. Because teachers did not focus instruction on writing about poetry, the lack of an intervention effect is not necessarily surprising. In addition, a student's writing ability is not likely to change in a matter of weeks (particularly when writing activities are secondary to think-and-feel-aloud instruction). Yet significant group differences between short-answer scores did emerge. (The short-answer responses served as more condensed versions of the informal essay responses that students wrote about a poem's possible meanings.) Scoring rules for short-answer responses focused narrowly on students' sentences and phrases, as they (a) addressed a poem's possible meanings and (b) specifically elaborated on those meanings. On the other hand, the essay rubric provided more general criteria for assigning a holistic score. Both scoring methods were highly reliable; nevertheless, the short-answer scores may indicate how well students could comment succinctly on a poem's possible meanings and support their answers. In addition, the informal essay may have prepared students to write a clearer, more condensed response to the question of meaning.

General Limitations of the Study

Of course, the study featured only two classrooms with relatively few student participants ($n = 40$). Certainly, a larger number of participants would further substantiate the positive influence of the think-and-feel-aloud intervention on readers' engagement with poetry and interpretative skills. In addition, experimental designs drawn from pre-established classroom cultures call into question the validity of a study where random group assignment cannot occur. However, statistical tests based on students' English grades and state test scores in reading and writing provided evidence of group equivalence.

Apart from the number of student participants and the way in which they were inevitably grouped, the study's internal validity might also be challenged based on instructor influence and bias. The students' literature teacher and the researcher collaboratively taught both groups to counter possible teacher effects. However, they were aware of the group conditions. Did they prompt the experimental group more? Analyses of the number of prompting questions teachers asked during classroom discussions indicated that there were not significant differences between groups (see Eva-Wood, 2003). In addition, because the researcher planned and proposed the experimental group instruction while the classroom teacher planned the control group instruction (his typical unit plan), they were able to keep each other in check—reading and engaging with the same materials in the same amount of time while varying instructional strategies and activities as appropriate. Furthermore, the classroom teacher had an obvious interest in making sure students in both classes were provided with quality instruction (a factor that might have worked to reduce differences between groups). Ideally, however, this study might be replicated in another set of classrooms with teachers who I train in the think-and-feel-aloud technique (vs. regular instruction).

Implications for Further Research

Study results indicate that the instructional intervention was effective in increasing students' interest in poetry and positively influencing their ability to analyze the texts they read. Assuming these links based on the data, a critical question remains: Why was the experimental intervention more effective? First of all, the instructional intervention based itself on the cognitive apprenticeship (A. Collins et al., 1989) model, which helps students to become aware of their own thinking as they solve problems (such as reading poetry). Therefore, think-aloud practices were featured to help students increase their metacognitive skills while reading. This component of instruction may have influenced students in the experimental group significantly.

However, the instructional design further expanded the cognitive apprenticeship model by incorporating affective response into a think-and-feel-aloud approach to reading. Students learned to use their initial affective responses as tools to help them understand the texts. This common practice in the experimental group may have played an equally powerful role. Further research might tease apart these influences in a study design that includes three conditions: a control, a think-aloud intervention, and a think-and-feel-aloud intervention. Regardless, the effects of the instructional intervention indicate that both think-aloud instruction and a focus on students' affective responses may help adolescent readers to enjoy and understand poetry.

Although some teachers argue that think alouds are useful in the class for literature discussions, understanding, and enjoyment (Oster, 2001), these assertions have not been tested scientifically. These findings provide evidence that increased metacognitive and metaemotive awareness may benefit student readers of poetry and other literature—perhaps even readers of nonliterary text types. Of course, this research also prompts the question of how much training is needed for these techniques to lead to changes in engagement and understanding. The students in the study presented here spent a month in either the control or TFA condition. Would only one example of modeling from the instructors paired with TFA instructions for reading a poem provide sufficient instruction to influence student engagement? Or is there some benefit to greater practice and exposure, as suggested by the study?

Furthermore, the qualitative analysis of classroom discussions indicates that students' emotional attentiveness to the speakers and characters in some poems serves as a powerful tool for interpretation. If students can be drawn into the emotional life of a character or speaker in a poem, they may be more likely to actively engage with poetry analysis. Further research in this area might focus more strategically on a variety of poetry types (i.e., with or without identifiable speakers, characters, settings, and story lines) to more narrowly explore the range of readers' affective responses. If students in the TFA condition readily respond to poems with sympathetic speakers, as this research suggests, teachers might also be more thoughtful about the types of poems they select to engage reluctant student readers.

The effects of the instructional intervention provide further evidence that cognitively driven, text-processing theories (e.g., Gernsbacher, 1990; Kintsch, 1988, 1998; van den Broek et al., 1999; Zwaan et al., 1995) can be enhanced with greater attention to the role affect plays in reading. In this study, adolescent readers who initially focused on their personal responses to texts seemed to participate more readily and thoughtfully with classroom reading materials. These findings might be extended to other literary texts such as narratives and novels. However, further research would be necessary to determine the generalizability of this instructional method to other literary and nonliterary text types.

CONCLUSION

The findings presented in this study indicate what most readers already know, but do not always practice. Explicit attention to both feelings and thoughts can lead to deeper, more meaningful responses to literature. Emotions and thoughts work interdependently to inform rich and complex poetic responses. However, because affect, even more than cognition, remains an often invisible and unconscious dimension of reading, the instructional intervention served to cue readers to become more aware of their affective responses as they read. Students in the experimental group learned to use their initial responses to poems as tools for further analysis.

To counter dispassionate, information processing models of reading, Wineburg (1994) described expert readers who give texts voices and engage those voices in conversation. These readings are both more palpably social and personal in quality (see also Wineburg, 1991). This research also endorses representations of readers conversing dynamically with texts, particularly when those readers are engaging poetry, which regularly upsets traditional textual conventions. Literary texts—and poems in particular—can propel readers to actively reorient to new rules and new ways of viewing the world. Because of the highly personal nature of literary reading, future theories must be reader driven—humanizing text processing without discarding the scientific approaches that can serve to ground theoretical conceptions of literary reading.

ACKNOWLEDGMENTS

Special thanks to Deborah McCutchen for her generous support and helpful advice on this study and to the reviewers for their thoughtful and informative editorial suggestions.

REFERENCES

Barthes, R. (1974). *S/Z.* New York: Hill & Wang.

Coleridge, S. T. (1983). *Biographia literaria* (2 Vols.) London: Routledge & Kegan Paul. (Original work published 1817)

Collins, A., Brown, J. S., & Newman, S. E. (1989). Cognitive apprenticeship: Teaching the crafts of reading, writing, and mathematics. In L. Resnick (Ed.), *Knowing, learning, and instruction: Essays in honor of Robert Glaser* (pp. 454–494). Hillsdale, NJ: Lawrence Erlbaum Associates, Inc.

Collins, B. (2001, November 23). The companionship of a poem. *The Chronicle of Higher Education,* p. B5.

Cupchik, G. C., Oatley, K., & Vorderer, P. (1992). Emotional effects of reading excerpts from short stories by James Joyce. *Poetics, 25,* 363–377.

Dadlez, E. M. (1997). *What's Hecuba to him? Fictional events and actual emotions.* University Park: Pennsylvania State University Press.

Dijkstra, K., Zwaan, R. A., Graesser, A. C., & Magliano, J. P. (1995). Character and reader emotions in literary texts. *Poetics, 23,* 139–157.

Earthman, E. A. (1992). Creating the virtual work: Reader's processes in understanding literary texts. *Research in the Teaching of English, 26,* 351–384.

Eva-Wood, A. (2003). Expanding the cognitive apprenticeship model: How a think-and-feel-aloud pedagogy influences poetry readers. *Dissertation Abstracts International, 64*(11), 3954. (UMI No. AAT3111061)

Feagin, S. (1996). *Reading with feeling: the aesthetics of appreciation.* Ithaca, NY: Cornell University Press.

Gernsbacher, M. A. (1990). *Language comprehension as structure building.* Hillsdale, NJ: Lawrence Erlbaum Associates, Inc.

Goetz, E. T., & Sadoski, M. (1996). Imaginative processes in literary comprehension. In R. J. Kreuz & M. S. MacNealy (Eds.), *Empirical approaches to literature and aesthetics* (pp. 221–240). Stamford, CT: Ablex.

Gutierrez, K. (1993, April). *Scripts, counterscripts, and multiple scripts.* Paper presented at the annual meeting of the American Educational Research Association, Atlanta.

Harker, W. J. (1994). "Plain sense and poetic significance": Tenth-grade readers reading two poems. *Poetics, 22,* 199–218.

Harley, H., & Ritter, L. (2002). Structuring the bundle: A universal morphosyntactic feature geometry. In H. J. Simon & H. Wiese (Eds.), *Pronouns—grammar and representation* (pp. 23–39). Philadelphia: Benjamins.

Heath, S. B. (1978). Teacher talk: Language in the classroom. *Language in Education: Theory and Practice, 1,* 1–30.

Hoffstaedter, P. (1987). Poetic text processing and its empirical investigation. *Poetics, 16,* 75–91.

Kintsch, W. (1988). The role of knowledge in discourse comprehension: A construction-integration model. *Psychological Review, 95,* 163–182.

Kintsch, W. (1998). *Comprehension: A paradigm for cognition.* New York: Cambridge University Press.

Kneepkens, E. W. E. M., & Zwaan, R. A. (1995). Emotions and literary text comprehension. *Poetics, 23,* 125–138.

Miall, D. S., & Kuiken, D. (1994). Beyond text theory: Understanding literary response. *Discourse Processes, 17,* 337–352.

Miall, D. S., & Kuiken, D. (1995). Aspects of literary response: A new questionnaire. *Research in the Teaching of English, 29,* 37–58.

Miall, D. S., & Kuiken, D. (2002). A feeling for fiction: Becoming what we behold. *Poetics, 30,* 221–241.

Mukarovsky, J. (1964). Standard language and poetic language. In P. L. Garvin (Ed.), *A Prague school reader on esthetics, literary structure, and style* (pp. 17–30). Washington, DC: Georgetown University Press. (Original work published 1932)

Nystrand, M. (1997). *Opening dialogue: Understanding the dynamics of language and learning in the English classroom.* New York: Teachers College Press.

Oster, L. (2001). Using the think-aloud for reading instruction. *The Reading Teacher, 55*(1), 64–69.

Peskin, J. (1998). Constructing meaning when reading poetry: An expert-novice study. *Cognition and Instruction, 16,* 235–263.

Pressley, M., & Afflerbach, P. (1995). *Verbal protocols of reading.* Hillsdale: NJ: Lawrence Erlbaum Associates, Inc.

Richards, I. A. (1929). *Practical criticism.* New York: Harcourt, Brace, and World.

Rosenblatt, L. M. (1995). *Literature as exploration* (5th ed.). New York: Modern Language Association of America.

Sarton, M. (1993). *May Sarton: Collected poems (1930–1993).* New York: Norton.

Shklovsky, V. (1965). Art as technique. In L. T. Lemon & M. J. Reis (Eds. & Trans.), *Russian formalist criticism: Four essays* (pp. 3–24). Lincoln: University of Nebraska Press. (Original work published 1917)

Strauss, A. L. (1987). *Qualitative analysis for social scientists.* Cambridge, England: Cambridge University Press.

van den Broek, P., Young, M., Tzeng, Y., & Linderholm, T. (1999). The landscape model of reading: Inferences and the online construction of a memory representation. In H. van Oostendorp & S. Goldman (Eds.), *The construction of mental representations during reading* (pp. 71–98). Mahwah, NJ: Lawrence Erlbaum Associates, Inc.

Vega, M., Leon, I., & Diaz, J. M. (1996). The representation of changing emotions in reading comprehension. *Cognition and Emotion, 10,* 303–322.

Wallace-Jones, J. (1991). Cognitive responses to poetry in 11 to 16 year olds. *Educational Review, 43,* 25–37.

Wineburg, S. S. (1991). On the reading of historical texts: Notes on the breach between school and the academy. *American Educational Research Journal, 28,* 495–519.

Wineburg, S. S. (1994). The cognitive representation of historical texts. In G. Leinhardt, I. L. Beck, & C. Stainton (Eds.), *Teaching and learning in history* (pp. 85–135). Hillsdale, NJ: Lawrence Erlbaum Associates, Inc.

Zwaan, R. A., Langston, M. C., & Graesser, A. C. (1995). The construction of situation models in narrative comprehension. *Psychological Review, 6,* 292–297.

DISCOURSE PROCESSES, *38*(2), 193–218

Foregrounding and Its Effect on Readers' Perception

Jèmeljan F. Hakemulder
Institute for Media and Representation
Utrecht University

There is an abundance of theory concerning the effects of reading literature. Some researchers do reveal effects, but few explain them. When they do, the textual features examined are neither necessary nor sufficient for literariness. Three experiments are presented here that study the relation between literary text quality and literary reading experience (aesthetic appreciation). The studies contrast effects of original literary texts and manipulated versions in which the degree of foregrounding found in the originals was minimized. To establish effects of foregrounding on literary reading experience, a rereading procedure was used. Results in part showed that foregrounding causes higher scores on aesthetic appreciation after participants read the texts a 2nd time. Furthermore, the literary texts revealed positive perception effects compared to nonforegrounding versions. These results suggest that foregrounding may enhance aesthetic appreciation and may be responsible for effects on perception.

Assumptions about the effects of reading literary texts are deeply rooted in Western concepts of literature. Definitions of what is typical of literature (Jakobson's *literariness*; see Stempel, 1972, p. 30) often generate empirical claims about the impact literary texts have on readers. It is assumed that readers may boost, among other things, their understanding of their fellow human beings and that it stimulates their reflection on moral dilemmas (Hakemulder, 2000). A number of experimental studies do indeed reveal that reading literature causes a wide range of effects (e.g., on empathic ability, moral development, critical thinking, outgroup perception, norms, and values). Few of these studies, however, examine whether the effects are particular to literature. Most researchers are primarily interested in establishing the value of using literature in educational settings (e.g., in programs

Correspondence and requests for reprints should be sent to Jèmeljan F. Hakemulder, Utrecht University, Kromme Nieuwegracht 29 3512HD Utrecht, The Netherlands. Email: j.hakemulder@let.uu.nl

aiming to reduce prejudice against outgroups) and do not include literary quality in their designs (e.g., Brisbin, 1971; Geiger, 1975; Hakemulder, 2000; Hermans & Hakemulder, 2003; Jackson, 1944; Litcher & Johnson, 1969; Tauran, 1967; Zucaro, 1972). Moreover, an obvious problem for assessing the effects of literature per se is the lack of a reliable measure for literariness. Because defining literariness is one of the central problems in literary theory, there are ample suggestions to solve this problem. One influential theory suggests that literature is characterized by deviations from daily language, or in other words, "the organized violence committed on ordinary speech" (Jakobson, as cited in Erlich, 1980, p. 219; Mukarovsky's, 1964, *foregrounding*; cf. also Shklovsky's, 1965, *devices*). As a result, readers' attention is focused on the form of the message instead of its content (Jakobson's, 1960, *poetic function*). This, in turn, would be followed by an effect on readers' perception. It would renew their awareness of the world around them. Because this theory couples specific text qualities with alleged effects of reading, it seems a suitable starting point for an empirical approach to the effects of literature. The studies presented in this article examine the effects of foregrounding, thus remedying the limited attention for literary text qualities in research.

Besides foregrounding theory, there are several other theories that explain the effects of literature on readers' perception. These can roughly be categorized in three groups: (a) those that propose that effects are caused by the content of literary texts, (b) those that stress the role of readers' identification with fictional characters, and (c) those that focus on the role of formal text aspects other than foregrounding.

As to content, some theorists say that, because some literary texts concern moral abuses in society or portray the moral dilemmas readers encounter in daily life, reading these texts can be expected to enhance ethical awareness (Nussbaum, 1991; Rushdie, 1991; Shelley, 1977; Steiner, 1989). Others suggest that readers perceive story plots as cause–effect scenarios and that exposure to such scenarios may affect their real-world beliefs and their expectations about their lives and about consequences of certain behaviors (Gardner, 1978; Zola, 1968). However, such contents are not exclusively found in literature, nor are all literary texts characterized by them. Other genres, like newspaper articles, may also enhance awareness of abuses in society, and philosophical essays may stimulate readers' ethical reflection. In addition, not all literary texts are concerned with moral issues, nor do they all have plots.

According to the first category of theories, content predicts effects. Various studies have shown that positive portrayals of outgroup members have positive effects on attitudes toward outgroups, whereas negative portrayals have negative effects (e.g., Brisbin, 1971; Geiger, 1975; Hakemulder, 2000; Hermans & Hakemulder, 2003; Jackson, 1944; Litcher & Johnson, 1969; Tauran, 1967; Zucaro, 1972). Researchers' estimates of moral reasoning levels in stimulus texts have been shown to predict the effectiveness of literature-based moral education programs (Biskin & Hoskisson, 1977; Gallager, 1978; Garrod, 1982; Johnson, 1990; Justice, 1989; Keefe, 1975; Kinnard, 1986). Comparing the effects of stories portraying egalitarian sex-roles with those of texts portraying nonegalitarian ones, some experimenters have shown that reading can affect sex-role concepts (Ashby & Wittmaier, 1978; Barclay, 1974; Berg-Cross & Berg-Cross, 1978; Flerx, Fidler, & Rogers, 1976; McArthur & Eisen, 1976). However, none of the evidence shows that these effects are actually due to the literary quality of the stimulus materials. Moreover, many of the narratives that were used in the experiments can be considered to be nonliterary texts.

The second category of theories proposes that by identifying with a character, readers enter an imaginary role-play (Booth, 1988). Thus, they learn about the consequences of certain behaviors and get a better understanding of what it must be like to be in someone else's shoes (Palmer, 1992; Rorty, 1989). Again, it should be noted that this factor is probably not exclusively associated with reading literature. It seems likely that identification can also occur when reading nonliterary texts. Studies that examine empathy as an experimental factor do show that boosting readers' role-taking behavior during reading enhances the effects of reading (e.g., Hakemulder, 2000, 2001; Schram & Geljon, 1988). In these studies, participants are asked to read an empathy-building instruction (cf. Bourg, Risden, Thompson, & Davis, 1993). This was found to affect perception of story characters, as well as perception of the social groups that they represent. But again, the results do not clarify the role of literary text qualities in the effects.

The third category of theories focuses on the role of formal text aspects other than foregrounding in the effects of literature. Some have suggested that moral messages are more persuasive when presented in the form of a good and exciting narrative rather than as straightforward moral laws (Egan, 1988; Horace, 1986). However, narrative form is neither a necessary nor a sufficient quality of literature. A number of studies do reveal the effectiveness of narrative form as compared to that of statistical evidence (for a review, see Reinard, 1988; see also Allen & Preiss's, 1997, meta-analysis, however, that contradicts this conclusion), but again, literariness is never a factor of interest.

To examine effects that are particular to literature clearly requires an empirical basis for literariness. Finding this will not be easy, as most attempts have been fiercely disputed. Some scholars and researchers argue that literary quality is determined by extratextual factors only. These include literary conventions, author and publisher status, and social dynamics of literary criticism (e.g., Fish, 1980; Herrnstein Smith, 1988; Schmidt, 1980, 1982; Verdaasdonk, 1983). For instance, in Fish's radical conventionalist view, every text (irrespective of form and content) can be perceived and interpreted as literature. Schmidt's radical constructivism led him to suggest that the study of literature's intrinsic qualities is fruitless. Instead, literary studies should focus on the four roles of the literary system: production, distribution, reception, and processing. Verdaasdonk argued that the quality that is attributed to a literary text depends not on intrinsic qualities (i.e., stylistic and compositional linguistic properties), but on the amount of attention that is given to this text by literary institutions such as publishing firms, literary criticism, literary theory, arts councils, and literature education. Herrnstein-Smith, on the other hand, claimed that the selection process resulting in the literary canon is and has always been ideological. In her view, the canon is an instrument to stabilize the political balance and to reproduce social inequality. In sum, many have proposed that it is impossible to determine text qualities that define literature. Literariness, they say, should rather be characterized in terms of reading strategies triggered by arbitrary conventions.

One objective of this contribution is to examine whether literariness can be defined by both textual factors (like foregrounding) and extratextual factors (like reader variables). It may therefore be more useful to speak of *literary reading experience* rather than *literariness*, a term generally associated with a set of text features that would describe literature in all situations and for all populations. Aesthetic preferences are clearly not identical for all readers (Bourdieu, 1984; Kraaykamp, 1993; van Rees, Vermunt, & Verboord, 1999). However, it is also unlikely that every text will generate literary reading experiences, as some theorists proposed (e.g., Fish, 1980). More probably, these experiences are sparked by distinct text qualities (e.g., foregrounding) and require readers to be able to realize the potential of these text qualities. Here, it is argued that, when this happens, it leads to an experience of aesthetic beauty and may result in changes in perception.

A possible objection against a focus on foregrounding is that it can be found in nonliterary texts as well, as Jakobson (1960) pointed out. However, Jakobson also argued that it is a text quality that is dominantly found in literature. Some empirical evidence confirms this assumption. Results of a linguistic study by van Peer (1986a) revealed systematically more obstruction (cf. Shklovsky, 1965) in a sample of literary texts as compared to a sample of popular texts. However, more important, focusing on literary reading experience generated by text qualities circumvents literary theorists' disputes over whether literature can be defined by foregrounding.

FOREGROUNDING

The theory of foregrounding can be traced back to the roots of literary theory—the school of the Russian Formalists at the beginning of the 20th century. Shklovsky (1965) argued that, by virtue of literary devices (he does not use the term *foregrounding* himself), reading literary texts restores people's sense of life. Their perception, Shklovsky suggested, is dulled by daily routine (*automatization*). This obliterates their feeling of being alive. Objects around them, their clothes, their furniture, their loved ones, their fear of war may disappear through this process of (over)familiarization. Literature defamiliarizes (e.g., through unusual metaphors and perspectives) and thus renews readers' awareness of the world around them. Shklovsky's ideas were further developed by the Czech Structuralists. Mukarovsky (1964) introduced the term *foregrounding*, defining it as a range of stylistic deviations that occur in literature—that is, deviations from the norms of everyday language. He distinguished three levels: (a) the phonetic level (e.g., alliteration, rhyme), (b) the grammatical level (e.g., inversion and ellipsis), and (c) the semantic level (e.g., metaphors, irony). Foregrounding makes readers focus primarily on style, not on content. This is not to say that literature does not have a communicative function. On the contrary, it is assumed that this mode of communication is more powerful than daily language. In sum, foregrounding theory assumes a relation between literary text qualities (deviations) and the effects on the reader (changes in perception).

The assumptions about the working of foregrounding are partly confirmed by experimental research. Some evidence points out that foregrounding plays a role in readers' reception of literary texts. Van Peer (1986b) found a relation between foregrounding and readers' interest. Participants were asked to read six poems and mark which lines seemed most striking to them. The results revealed a strong consensus. Moreover, van Peer reported a significant correlation between participants' ranking of strikingness and his scoring of foregrounding prior to the experiment. These results proved to be independent of participants' levels of literary training.

Besides readers' interest, evidence shows an influence of foregrounding on text processing and affect. In a study by Miall and Kuiken (1994), participants read one of three selected stories. Each story was presented on a computer screen in segments of about 20 words. Prior to the experiment, three independent researchers analyzed the stories, determining the degree of foregrounding in each segment. Participants first read their assigned text in a self-paced reading time experiment whereby text segments were presented on the screen and readers pressed for subsequent segments. A second time participants read the text, they were asked to rate each segment on a number of scales measuring perceived strikingness, affect, importance, and discussion value. The results revealed a significant correlation between the degree of foregrounding and reading time: The more foregrounding, the slower readers read the text. This suggests foregrounding causes a more thorough processing of the text. Moreover, it was found that degree of foregrounding correlated positively with ratings on strikingness and levels of reported affect. The results were again independent of participants' literary background and interest.

One objective of the study presented here is to extend the findings of van Peer (1986b) and Miall and Kuiken (1994). As discussed earlier, the claims of literary theory go beyond reception variables (e.g., strikingness). To test these claims, the study presented here examines whether foregrounding can be responsible for the effects on perception of things other than the text itself.

REREADING PARADIGM

This investigation builds on research by Dixon, Bortolussi, Twilley, and Leung (1993). In their procedure, participants are asked to read a text twice and rate their appreciation of it after each reading. Dixon et al. assumed that literary texts are more complex than other genres, such as detective novels. Literary effects, there-fore, develop over time in multiple readings of the text. A concept central to the paradigm is *depth of appreciation*—that is, the increase in appreciation from the first evaluation to the second. For literary texts, Dixon et al. expected an increase in appreciation. Such an effect is not expected from rereading a nonliterary text. However, literariness, they proposed, can only be the product of an interaction be-tween reader and text; the effect of the text depends on whether a certain popula-tion recognizes the text features as literary devices.

In their first experiment, they used two stories—one by Borges and a so-called true detective story from a popular magazine. When comparing partici-pants' first and second evaluation, the researchers found that only the responses to the Borges story revealed a significant increase of appreciation. In their sec-ond experiment, Dixon et al. (1993) tried to determine the text feature responsi-ble for this effect. After close examination of Borges' story, they proposed that it may be its ambiguous narrator, a factor significant to their own interpretation of the text. At many points in the story, the narrator seems poorly informed about events in the fictional world. He sometimes does not know exactly where the main character is, what she is doing, and what her emotions and motives are (cf. Shklovsky's, 1965, idea of obstruction of readers' perception of the fictional world). This leaves readers guessing, too. Presumably, it gets them more in-volved in the construction of the story (cf. Iser, 1970). The researchers manipu-lated both texts, neutralizing the ambiguity of the Borges text and rewriting the crime story by changing its omniscient narrator into a more ambiguous one. Fre-quent readers revealed a greater depth of appreciation for the Borges story, but not for the version without the ambiguous narrator, suggesting that the ambigu-ity must have played an important role in their appreciation of the story. In the detective story, the manipulation had hardly any effect. For infrequent readers, a greater depth of appreciation was also found for the Borges story, but results showed no effects for narrator ambiguity.

In another study (Hakemulder, van Peer, & Zyngier, 2003), these findings were extended. The researchers independently rated 10 extracts from British and Amer-ican literature on degree of complexity. Three texts were selected, one with a low level (popular romance novel), one with a medium level (Jane Austen), and one with a high level (Virginia Woolf) of complexity. After a rereading procedure, re-sponses to the most complex text revealed more depth of appreciation than those to the least complex text. Again, this effect proved to be mediated by reported reading frequency.

The rereading procedure seems to provide the necessary means to assess the interaction between text and reader variables in the production of literary reading experiences. It should be noted, however, that this approach does not rule out the possibility that, for some readers, it may be pleasurable to reread, as might be the case for, say, a popular novel. Neither does this approach suggest that a text is only literary when it is reread or that literary text qualities are readers' sole motive for wanting to reread texts. Furthermore, it is possible that some readers read a literary text without realizing its literary potential and, therefore, without having a literary reading experience. However, focusing on such variations in responses to different types of texts may provide an empirical basis for literariness (or rather literary experience). While taking into consideration that reader variables may intervene, it can be assumed that appreciation of literary texts increases after second reading, whereas rereading nonliterary texts will not have this effect. It seems likely that an understanding of most of the literary devices in the text will only emerge after closer examination. Considering the results of Dixon et al. (1993), a rereading procedure may be assumed to stimulate this process.

THE RESEARCH PRESENTED HERE

Can the rereading studies by Dixon et al. (1993) and Hakemulder et al. (2003) be interpreted as supporting foregrounding theory? The manipulated text factor in Dixon et al.'s experiments is clearly a foregrounding text feature. The ambiguous narrator in the original text that researchers used obstructs readers' understanding of the fictional events and deviates from what readers may expect from narrators. However, in the Hakemulder et al. study, researchers' rating of complexity cannot be related to distinct text qualities. Because of this lack of control, results cannot be seen as direct support for foregrounding theory. In the studies presented here, it is examined whether a more controlled procedure would result in more evidence for the effects of foregrounding. To do this, a rereading procedure will be used. The prediction is that foregrounding is, besides narrator ambiguity and complexity, a likely source of the phenomenon Dixon at al. called depth of appreciation.

The results of van Peer (1986b) and Miall and Kuiken (1994) may lead to the expectation that the depth of appreciation Dixon et al. (1993) attributed to narrator ambiguity will also, in the case of foregrounding, be accompanied by other effects. Their studies indicated effects on participants' ratings on strikingness, interest, and affect. To extend these findings, the studies presented here examined whether foregrounding can generate literary reading experiences. It was tested whether a second reading of a text with a high level of foregrounding causes a larger increase in aesthetic appreciation than a similar text with a lower level of foregrounding. In addition, it was examined whether a text with a high level of foregrounding has a stronger effect on readers' perception than a text with a lower level of foregrounding. The experiments used original literary texts as well as manipulated versions in which the degree of foregrounding was minimized. A pilot study tested the effects of foregrounding in a literary text read by sociology students. The study was run again with literature students in Experiment 1 to investigate the possible role of subject variables. Experiment 2 improves on the first—among other things, in the higher degree to which foregrounding was manipulated.

PILOT STUDY

The general purpose of the pilot study was to relate one particular approach to literariness to the effects of reading on perception. It is examined whether depth of appreciation—that is, the increase of appreciation between first and second reading of a text—can be caused by foregrounding. If degree of foregrounding is responsible for variations in depth of appreciation, would this also help to predict the relative effect these texts may have on perception?

METHOD

Participants

The experiment was conducted at Utrecht University. Participants were college freshmen sociology students ($N = 32$; 6 men, 26 women; ages ranging from 18 to 22, $M = 18.90$, $SD = 1.22$). They were asked to participate in the experiment as an introduction to experimental research.

Materials

The Dutch translation of the beginning of Rushdie's (1988) *The Satanic Verses* (600 words) was selected because it was assumed that participants were aware of the various issues regarding immigrants described in the text. Two text sections were chosen: the opening of the novel describing how the two main characters, both Indian immigrants, fall down from an airplane and miraculously land safely on one of Britain's snowy beaches, and a second section describing how policemen, hunting for illegal immigrants as if they were animals, falsely arrest one of the two characters. The two sections were interlaced by a brief summary to ensure coherence.

Rushdie's text is very baroque. It consists of long and complicated sentences full of extraordinary metaphors, some referring to the position of immigrants in their new "home country." Following a procedure similar to Dixon et al.'s (1993), the text was rewritten by the experimenter, deleting most of its foregrounding (see Table 1).

TABLE 1
Manipulation of Rushdie's Text

Original text	The aircraft cracked in half, a seed-pod giving up its spores, an egg yielding its mystery. Two actors, prancing Gibreel and buttony, pursed Mr. Saladin Chamcha, fell like titbits of tobacco from a broken old cigar. Above, behind, below them in the void there hung reclining seats, stereophonic headsets, drink trolleys, motion discomfort receptacles, disembarkation cards, duty-free video games, braided caps, paper cups, blankets, oxygen masks. Also–for there had been more than a few migrants aboard, yes, quite a quantity of wives who had been grilled by reasonable, doing-their-job officials about the length of and distinguishing moles upon their husbands' genitalia, a sufficiency of children upon whose legitimacy the British Government had cast its ever-reasonable doubts.
Manipulation	After the explosion the airplane broke in two. The two actors, Djibriel and Saladin Chamcha fell down. Everywhere around them objects were floating. There had been many migrants on board. Among whom many women. Before their departure they had been questioned about intimate details about their husbands. Besides them there were many children on board, about whose legitimate status the British Government also had had their doubts.

Note. Texts were presented in Dutch. This example is taken from the original Rushdie (1988) publication in English, whereas that of the manipulated version is a translation back into English by the researcher.

Clearly, the second text, a mere paraphrase or summary of the first, has a lower degree of foregrounding: The length of the sentences is shorter. The enumeration of floating objects (reclining seats through to oxygen masks) is deleted in the manipulation, as were the unusual metaphors (e.g., the comparison of the plane with a broken cigar). The more sober summary also lacks ironic adjectives such as *doing-their-job* and *ever-reasonable*. It seems obvious that this aspect foregrounds the (implied) author's message. Therefore, it may be expected that the original version has a stronger effect on readers' perception of the position of outgroups in the West than the manipulated version, although the events described are the same. It could be argued that there is still some foregrounding left in the manipulated version (e.g., the curious story events themselves). However, the manipulation of form was carried out as far as possible, keeping in mind that the content of the original and the manipulated version had to be similar. Moreover, for the purpose of this study, it sufficed to have a considerable difference in degree of foregrounding in the two texts.

Procedure

Participants were randomly assigned to one of three groups: two experimental groups that each read one of the two texts and one control group. They were told that the researcher was interested in their responses to literature. The experiment was based on the rereading paradigm to establish the degree to which the stimulus material would generate a literary experience. Participants of the two experimental groups read their assigned text twice and responded to the three appreciation scales reported in Dixon et al. (1993) on 7-point scales ranging from 1 (*no*) to 7 (*yes*): (a) "Do you think this is an example of good literature?," (b) "Did you enjoy reading the text?" (instead of "story" in the Dixon questionnaire), and (c) "Would you recommend this text to someone else to read?" One question was added, "Would you be interested to read the rest of this story?" as an extra indicator of participants' appreciation of the texts.

After reading the texts, the two experimental groups filled out an opinion test that consisted of 14 statements concerning the position of immigrants in Western Europe. The same test was administered to the control group. The task was presented to the participants as an experimental control measure for the assessment of their text appreciation. All participants were asked to indicate on a 7-point scale ranging from 1 (*totally disagree*) to 7 (*totally agree*) to which degree they agreed with the statements. Four scales were constructed: (a) beliefs about how serious the difficulties of immigrants are when trying to adapt to their new environment and to feel at home; (b) beliefs about the extent of discrimination, unfriendliness, and intolerance immigrants meet in their new environment; (c) beliefs about the low level of acceptance among indigenous population that immigrants encounter; and (d) beliefs about immigrants' motives for coming to the West, or, more in particular, whether they come out of necessity rather than free will. These issues were selected because they correspond with the themes in the stimulus material. It was expected that, as compared to the control group, readers of the original Rushdie text would score higher on all scales (indicating more severe conditions for immigrants in the West) than the readers of the manipulated version. A week after the experiment, participants were debriefed and informed about the results of the study.

RESULTS AND DISCUSSION

First, a repeated-measure multivariate analysis of variance (MANOVA) was conducted on the individual appreciation items, with appreciation scores after first versus second reading as a within-subject measure and original versus manipulated version as a between-subjects measure. Participants' age and gender were used as covariates in the analysis. This did not reveal any significant effect or any interactions (see Table 2). Scores on first and second reading in both conditions were approximately the same.

Second, it was examined whether exposure to the texts had influenced readers' opinions about immigrants. Reliability analyses were conducted on the four opinion scales. All tests revealed alphas above .85. In subsequent analyses, these scales were used to study effects of the texts on participants' opinions. To do this, a

TABLE 2
Average Scores on Text Evaluation in the Rereading Procedure:
Pilot (Sociology) and Experiment 1 (Literature)

	Condition							
	High Foregrounding				Low Foregrounding			
	First Reading		Second Reading		First Reading		Second Reading	
Question	M	SD	M	SD	M	SD	M	SD
Pilot								
Is this good literature?	2.67	1.37	2.67	1.37	1.75	1.34	2.03	1.42
Did you enjoy it?	2.42	1.83	2.53	1.72	2.39	1.41	2.32	1.25
Recommend to a friend?	1.42	1.56	1.42	1.62	1.81	1.45	1.74	1.36
Want to read on?	2.25	2.18	2.08	2.06	2.71	1.62	2.55	1.67
Experiment 1								
Is this good literature?	2.55	1.62	3.78	1.31	1.74	1.34	2.03	1.42
Did you enjoy it?	2.17	1.79	3.17	1.34	2.39	1.41	2.32	1.25
Recommend to a friend?	2.11	1.71	2.06	1.59	1.81	1.45	1.74	1.36
Want to read on?	2.94	1.95	3.67	1.68	2.71	1.62	2.55	1.67

MANOVA was run, with the four opinion scales as dependent variables and condition (control vs. readers of the original text vs. readers of the manipulated version) as the independent variable. This did not reveal any significant effects, suggesting that neither the original nor the manipulated version had an effect on participants' perception (see Table 3). The results hardly show any differences between control group average scores and those of the experimental groups.

TABLE 3
Average Scores on Perception Measures:
Pilot (Sociology) and Experiment 1 (Literature)

| | Condition | | | | | |
| | Control | | High Foregrounding | | Low Foregrounding | |
Belief Scales	M	SD	M	SD	M	SD
Pilot						
Adaptation problems	4.87	0.85	4.71	1.05	4.25	1.52
Intolerance	3.44	1.03	3.61	1.01	4.20	0.93
Low acceptance	4.05	1.27	3.58	1.24	4.67	0.83
Necessity	4.82	1.15	5.21	0.99	4.23	1.56
Experiment 1						
Adaptation problems	4.58	1.03	4.69	1.05	4.93	0.75
Intolerance	3.45	0.78	4.16	0.79	3.75	0.93
Low acceptance	4.20	0.98	4.56	0.95	4.27	1.23
Necessity	4.00	1.54	4.00	1.37	4.25	1.15

Discussion

In sum, for this sample, the manipulation of foregrounding did not affect participants' literary reading experience. Average appreciation scores on first and second reading remained more or less the same for both texts. Neither of the two texts seemed to have affected participants' opinions.

As proposed earlier, it is possible that literary reading experiences (e.g., aesthetic pleasure and changes in perception) do not depend solely on textual features, but that they emerge as the result of an interaction between reader and text. For one group of readers, rereading a literary text may result in new insights in the text or "renewed awareness"; for another, it may not. In the studies by Dixon et al. (1993) and Hakemulder et al. (2003), it was found that emergent effects depend on reported reading frequency. Also, the Sociology students may not have been familiar with complex literary texts like Rushdie's. This may be why effects on appreciation and perception did not occur. To examine this possibility, the experiment was rerun, but this time with participants who are trained in reading and analyzing literary texts.

EXPERIMENT 1

Purpose

The purpose of this experiment was to examine whether the predicted effects of foregrounding would be found when the study was conducted with participants with literary training.

METHOD

Participants

The experiment was conducted at Utrecht University. Participants were college freshmen literary studies students ($N = 60$; 14 men, 46 women; ages ranging from 18 to 39, $M = 20.32$, $SD = 3.07$). They were asked to participate in the experiment as an introduction to empirical studies of literature.

Procedure

Participants were randomly assigned to three groups: two experimental groups and one control group. The same materials and method as in the pilot study were used. For practical reasons, it was run during one session instead of conducting the experiment in smaller groups of about 10 participants, as in the pilot study.

RESULTS AND DISCUSSION

Appreciation

The results of first and second reading text evaluations were analyzed using repeated measures MANOVAs (appreciation on first vs. second reading, original vs. manipulated text), with age and gender as covariates. This revealed significant interactions for participants' scores on "Do you think this is an example of good literature?" $F(1, 49) = 4.97, p < .05, MSE = 1.62$; on "Did you enjoy reading the text?" $F(1, 49) = 7.03, p < .05, MSE = 1.54$; and on one interaction effect approaching significance for "Would you be interested to read the rest of this story?" $F(1, 49) = 4.00, p = .052, MSE = 1.85$. As to perceived literary quality, results show an increase in scores for the Rushdie group ($M = 2.55, SD = 1.62$ on first reading, and $M = 3.78, SD = 1.31$ on second reading) and only a small increase among readers of the manipulated version ($M = 1.74, SD = 1.34$ on first reading, and $M = 2.03, SD = 1.42$ on second reading; see Table 2). Bonferroni post hoc analyses were conducted to see whether the changes for the individual text groups were significant. As to perceived literary quality, the rise registered for the original Rushdie text was significant at the .05 level. No effect was found for the changes in appreciation for the manipulated version. As to enjoyment, in the Rusdhie group, there is an increase in scores ($M = 2.17, SD = 1.79$ on first reading, and $M = 3.17, SD = 1.34$ on second reading). In the group that read the manipulated version, scores remain approximately equal ($M = 2.39, SD = 1.41$ on first reading, and $M = 2.32, SD = 1.25$ on second reading). Post hoc analysis revealed that the changes in reported enjoyment of the individual groups were not significant. Results for "Would you be interested to read the rest of this story?" show an increase in scores for the readers of Rushdie's original text ($M = 2.94, SD = 1.95$ on first reading, and $M = 3.67, SD = 1.68$ on second reading) and a small decrease in scores for the readers of the manipulated version ($M = 2.71, SD = 1.62$ on first reading, and $M = 2.55, SD = 1.67$ on second reading). However, post hoc analysis revealed no significant changes within the individual groups. Finally, no significant interactions were found on "Would you recommend this text to someone else to read?" In sum, the manipulation did affect literary reading experience, but they were restricted to three of the four registered aspects only: perceived literary quality, enjoyment, and readers' interest in reading the rest of the text.

Perception

It was examined whether reading either of the two texts had an impact on readers' beliefs about immigrants. In the analysis, the results of the two experimental groups and the control group were compared. A MANOVA was conducted on the data for the four opinion scales (all alphas above .77). This revealed significant effects for condition on two of the four scales: intolerance, $F(3, 60) = 9.91, p < .001$, $MSE = .73$; and low acceptance, $F(3, 60) = 2.86, p < .05, MSE = 1.04$. A simple planned contrast revealed that only the scores of the original Rushdie readers on intolerance ($M = 4.16, SD = .79$; see Table 3) differ significantly from the control group scores ($M = 3.45, SD = .78$; Rushdie manipulated: $M = 3.75, SD = .93$). The effect was in the predicted direction: Readers of Rushdie's original text considered intolerance toward migrants significantly more severe than the control group participants did. However, planned contrasts for the low-acceptance scale revealed no significant differences. Neither the original Rushdie text nor its manipulated version seemed to have affected participants' scores. In addition, the results show that none of the contrasts for the manipulated Rushdie group were significant.

Discussion

It can be concluded that the manipulation of foregrounding caused significant differences in emergent effects between the two texts. Also, foregrounding caused small but significant effects on participants' perception.

One of the problems of the study presented here is the low appreciation scores for the stimulus material. This may have to do with the extravagant style of Rushdie that few of the participants may have appreciated. Scores on the question "Would you be interested to read the rest of this story" were affected by the manipulation, but they were also very low (for the high-foregrounding text, $M = 2.25, SD = 2.18$ on first reading, and $M = 2.08, SD = 2.06$ on second reading; and for the low-foregrounding text: $M = 2.71, SD = 1.62$ on first reading, and $M = 2.55, SD = 1.67$ on second reading). It may be suggested that the significant results on the appreciation items are merely due to an increase in text comprehension on second reading. One of the aims of Experiment 2 was to examine this possibility, using additional measures to assess changes in participants' understanding of the text.

In Experiment 2, a much simpler and therefore possibly more appealing text was used—Nabokov's (1996) poem "The Old Bridge." An additional advantage is that this short text can be presented completely, whereas in the pilot and Experiment 1, fragments had to be used, possibly reducing coherence. The poem consists of 64 words, and therefore, it seems it would be easier for participants' to take a view of the whole text and grasp its structure. Also, Nabokov's text could be manipulated to a higher degree than the Rushdie text. In the latter, the peculiar story events had to be maintained. Changing Nabokov's poetry into low-foregrounding prose is less complicated.

It may be that participants in Experiment 1 (and the pilot study) sensed that their tasks were related. The sharp irony of the Rushdie text may have enticed them to respond to the opinion questionnaire in a way that they considered appropriate. Experiment 2 focused on concepts of love, effects that may be less susceptible to social desirability. As in the two previous experiments, it can be assumed that the theme was not new to them. It was probably not the first time participants will be confronted with concepts of love. The measures were aimed at registering changes in their personal concepts.

EXPERIMENT 2

Purpose

Experiment 2 was conducted to solve some of the problems that occurred in Experiment 1. A simpler text, Nabokov's (1996) poem "The Old Bridge," was used and was expected to yield higher scores on appreciation than the Rushdie text used in the previous experiments. In addition, it is a text that could be presented to participants in its entirety and that could be manipulated to a higher degree than the selected sections from *The Satanic Verses* (Rushdie, 1988). Additional measures were taken to enhance control over reader variables, text comprehension, and readers' responses to the rereading procedure itself.

METHOD

Participants

Participants in this experiment were 60 art students from Utrecht University (48 women and 11 men, 1 case missing; ages 19 to 25, $M = 20.56$, $SD = 1.20$, 1 case missing). They entered an introductory course to Psychological Approaches to Theater, Film, and Television Studies. As part of the course, they were asked to participate in a study to familiarize themselves with experimental procedures. The group of 60 was part of a larger group of students who all participated in a number of experiments run simultaneously. All students were randomly assigned to one of five conditions, only three of which are relevant here: one control group and two experimental groups.

Materials

The first experimental group read Nabokov's poem. This time, the stimulus materials were presented to the Dutch participants in English because the texts are relatively easy to understand. Using the English text, furthermore, has the advantage that participants could be presented with the original foregrounding of the poem. The second experimental group read the manipulated version of the poem without the foregrounding.

Based on an interpretation by the experimenter, three levels of interpretation were distinguished in the original. The first is basic text comprehension (the events of the narrative). At sunset, two people stand on an old bridge and see a swift flying by. The narrator asks his companion whether she will ever forget this moment, and she passionately replies that she never will. When trying to interpret the text further, readers may come to the conclusion that the poem concerns the nature of love. Certain aspects seem to point out to readers that love is an eternal feeling. It has a circular structure, ending with the same image of the old bridge at sunset, which seems to keep readers with the poem forever, thus, as it where, fulfilling its own promise of eternity. Moreover, the characters state themselves that the moment they share should and will be remembered forever. A third interpretation level, however, seems to hint at the transitory nature of love. One of the lines paradoxically states that the moment will be remembered "till we die, till tomorrow, forever." The combination of "till we die" and "forever" on the one hand, and "till tomorrow" on the other, seems to foreground the fact that the feelings the two have may not be everlasting at all. The soft irony that readers may perceive in the poem seems to foreground the overly sentimental mood the two people are in. The river that runs under the bridge can be interpreted as a metaphor for transitoriness. The same holds for the swift—a very speedy bird. The word *swift* itself has the alternate meaning of *quick*.

It may be suggested, along the lines of foregrounding theory, that stating in plain language that love is not eternal does not have the same impact as reading and reflecting on the interpretation of Nabokov's poem. Readers' discovery of the significance of the literary devices and their interrelation can be assumed to add to their initial aesthetic appreciation (i.e., an admiration for how well the text is structured).

The experimenter's manipulation of the original version of the poem was aimed at removing all its foregrounding. Logically incorrect expressions were simplified or neutralized. More current words replaced low-frequency ones. The punctuation missing in the original was added in the new version. Repetition in the original poem was omitted in the manipulation, thus eliminating, among other things, its circular structure. Words with double meanings were replaced by less ambiguous ones (e.g., *bird* replaced *swift*). Consequently, rereading this text was not expected to reveal any literary devices at work and would not lead readers to any of the interpretations proposed here—neither on the second level (an expression of eternal love) nor on the third (the transitory nature of love). It was predicted, therefore, that rereading the manipulated version would not result in a higher aesthetic appreciation nor that it would affect perception.

Measures

Appreciation of the text after first and second reading was measured using the same questionnaire (in Dutch translation, with some minor adjustments) as used in Dixon et al. (1993): (a) "Do you think this is an example of good literature?" (b) "Did you enjoy reading the poem?" (instead of "story" in the Dixon questionnaire), and (c) "Would you recommend this poem to someone else to read?" The fourth item was irrelevant for this study and therefore dropped. All questions were answered on 7-point scales ranging from 1 (*definitely is not good literature, definitely did not enjoy, definitely would not recommend*) to 7 (*definitely is good literature, definitely did enjoy, definitely would recommend*).

In addition, a number of questions were put to the participants after both the first and second readings to assess perceived complexity. Participants were asked to answer the following questions: (a) "Did you have any trouble understanding the poem?" (b) "Do you think this poem has more than one level of interpretation?" (c) "To what extent do you feel the poem was intentionally ambiguous?" and (d) "To what extent did the author imply things that weren't explicitly stated?"

After second reading, participants were asked to answer three additional questions to assess whether they were aware of any "emergent effects" themselves: (a) "To what extent did you perceive new aspects of the poem the second time around?" (b) "Was rereading the poem enjoyable?" and (c) "Do you think you would get more out of a third reading?"

To assess effects on perception, all participants were asked to think of the concept of love and indicate on a 7-point semantic differential which of two adjectives fit their own concept best. This task was presented to the participants as an association test that the experimenter had been asked to conduct for a foreign colleague. The measure was used in an earlier study by the experimenter and consisted of a number of adjective pairs that were expected to reveal differences in responses to the Nabokov poem: (a) fragile–strong, (b) dark–light, (c) helpless–powerful, (d) melancholic–lighthearted, (e) predictable–surprising, (f) painful–happy, (g) slow–fast, (h) temporal–permanent, (i) despondent–comforting, (j) sad–merry, (k) fleeting–lasting, (l) weak–powerful, and (m) heavy–airy. It was predicted that, given the nature of the adjectives, especially (h) and (k), the data would reveal that the Nabokov poem affected participants' perception of love, and the manipulated version would not.

Comparing the results of Experiment 1 and those of the pilot study, it was expected that the effects of foregrounding would be mediated by reading frequency. Therefore, participants were asked to indicate how much time they had spent reading in the week before the experiment.

Procedure

The control group consisted of participants assigned to one of the conditions of another experiment that was run simultaneously. Prior to their actual task, they were asked to fill out the association test. Participants of the two experimental conditions were asked to read the text, respond to the evaluation questions and the questions pertaining to perceived complexity, reread the text, and answer the same questions again. Finally, they responded to additional questions assessing awareness of emergent effects and filled out the association test. A week later, they were debriefed and informed about the results of the study.

RESULTS AND DISCUSSION

Appreciation

Repeated measures MANOVAs were run, with scores on the rereading appreciation items (pretest vs. posttest) as a within-subject variable and text (the high-fore-grounding vs. its low-foregrounding version) as a between-subjects factor. Age and gender were entered as covariates. Considering the different results for the pilot (sociology students) and Experiment 1 (literature students), it would have been interesting to enter reading frequency as an independent variable. To do this, the sample was divided into two approximately equal groups of (a) high-frequency readers (those reporting to have read 4 or more hours in the week before the experiment) and (b) low-frequency readers (3 and less hours). However, running the MANOVAs, some of the cells proved to be too small to allow a meaningful interpretation of the results. Therefore, reading frequency was used in subsequent analyses as a covariate.

On one of the three rereading items assessing emergent appreciation effects ("Did you enjoy reading the poem?"), there was a significant interaction between the repeated measure and the text that was read, $F(1, 43) = 4.28$, $p < .05$, $MSE = 1.70$. The data of the high-foregrounding group reveal an increase in average scores ($M = 4.78$, $SD = 1.37$ on first reading, and $M = 5.30$, $SD = 1.26$ on second reading; see Table 4). Also, it may be important to note that average scores are con-

TABLE 4
Average Scores on Text Evaluation
in the Rereading Procedure: Experiment 2

	Condition							
	High Foregrounding				Low Foregrounding			
	First Reading		Second Reading		First Reading		Second Reading	
Questions	M	SD	M	SD	M	SD	M	SD
Appreciation								
Is this good literature?	4.70	1.14	5.00	1.18	3.94	1.34	3.94	1.12
Did you enjoy it?	4.78	1.37	5.30	1.26	4.37	1.45	3.93	1.57
Recommend to a friend?	4.29	1.31	4.71	1.49	3.56	1.71	3.43	1.63
Perceived complexity								
Trouble understanding?	2.52	1.34	2.92	1.33	2.12	1.15	2.56	1.41
More than one level?	4.88	1.53	5.47	1.07	4.69	1.70	5.00	1.71
Intentionally ambiguous?	4.58	1.12	5.23	0.97	4.37	1.67	4.56	1.82
Implicit?	5.18	0.88	5.18	0.95	4.31	1.30	4.31	1.78

siderably higher here than in the pilot and Experiment 1 (see Table 2). Low appreciation (like for the Rushdie text) may hinder emergent effects. If so, it seems less likely that the Nabokov poem would cause such problems. In the group that read the manipulated version, scores decreased ($M = 4.37$, $SD = 1.45$ after first reading, and $M = 3.93$, $SD = 1.57$ after second reading). Post hoc analyses revealed that, although there was a significant interaction, changes within the individual groups were not significant at the .05 level. Results of the MANOVAs run on the two other items ("Do you think this is an example of good literature?" and "Would you recommend this poem to someone else to read?") did not reveal any significant main effects or any interaction effects. No effects were found for the covariates (including reported reading frequency).

Awareness of Emergent Effects

MANOVAs were run on the items that indicate participants' awareness of emergent effects. This revealed significant effects on all three. Readers of the original poem scored significantly higher, $F(1, 43) = 4.83$, $p < .05$, $MSE = 2.40$, on the question "To what extent did you perceive new aspects of the story the second time around?" ($M = 3.78$, $SD = 1.58$) than readers of the manipulated version ($M = 2.62$, $SD = 1.36$). Similarly, scores on "Was rereading the poem enjoyable?" revealed significantly higher scores, $F(1, 43) = 6.51$, $p < .05$, $MSE = 2.29$, for the Nabokov readers ($M = 4.81$, $SD = 1.44$) than for the readers of the manipulated version ($M = 3.75$, $SD = 1.61$). Also, on the third question, "Do you think you would get more out of a third reading?" significantly higher scores, $F(1, 43) = 4.68$, $p < .05$, $MSE = 2.86$, were registered for the Nabokov group ($M = 4.37$, $SD = 1.67$) than readers of the manipulated version ($M = 3.06$, $SD = 1.65$). Again, no effects were found for reported reading frequency and the other covariates.

Perceived Complexity

To estimate whether text comprehension can be seen as an emergent effect that may in part be responsible for other emergent effects (in this case, enjoyment), the responses to questions pertaining to perceived complexity were analyzed. Repeated measures MANOVAs revealed no significant differences. After second reading, participants did not report finding the text easier to understand. Nor did they report detecting more of the text's ambiguity, implicitness, or extra levels of interpretation (see Table 4).

Perception

A factor analysis was run (principal components, Varimax rotation, eigenvalues above 1) on the items of the association test. Four components were extracted (see Table 5). One factor was extracted with an eigenvalue of 4.1, explaining 31% of the

TABLE 5
Factor Loadings on the Love Association Test Items

Items	Factors			
	1	*2*	*3*	*4*
Fragile–strong	**.65**	.07	.06	.31
Dark–light	.12	**.58**	.02	.50
Helpless–powerful	.11	**.78**	.02	.17
Melancholic–lighthearted	.12	.04	**.74**	.05
Predictable–surprising	.01	.10	.02	**.86**
Painful–happy	.39	**.70**	.21	.29
Slow–fast	.03	.20	**.68**	.25
Temporal–permanent	**.87**	.06	.03	.02
Despondent–comforting	.32	**.61**	.35	.00
Sad–merry	.18	**.66**	.43	.10
Fleeting–lasting	**.78**	.21	.00	.11
Weak–powerful	**.67**	.24	.33	.05
Heavy–airy	.03	.26	**.72**	.26

Note. Loadings in bold indicate items included in the factors.

variance: fragile–strong, temporal–permanent, fleeting–lasting, and weak–powerful. A second factor yielded an eigenvalue of 1.8 (14% explained variance): dark–light, helpless–powerful, painful–happy, despondent–comforting, and sad–merry. A third factor had an eigenvalue of 1.6, explaining 12% of the variance: melancholic–lighthearted, slow–fast, and heavy–airy. Finally, the fourth factor (eigenvalue of 1.0, explaining 7.7%) yielded only one item: predicable–surprising. Considering the interpretation of the poem presented previously, the first factor seems to fit the purpose of this study closest. It may be labeled *eternal love*. It was expected that readers of the original text would score lower on eternal love than the readers of the manipulated version. This would indicate that the latter stuck to the second level of interpretation (expressing eternal love), whereas the former had discovered the third level (expressing that feelings of eternal love are transitory). The second factor seems interpretable, too, and may also be used to examine the effect of the poem. It may be that the readers would not discover the suggested third interpretation level of the poem. Possibly, they recognize some of the foregrounding that was discussed, but only those aspects that lead to the second level of interpretation. To test this assumption, it may be interesting to look at the results for the second interpretable factor as well, which can be labeled *power of love*. The two other factors were not used in the analyses because they do not seem to have any relevance to the purpose of this study.

    To test the effect of the poems, a MANOVA was conducted with scores on the two factors (eternal love and power of love) as the dependent variable and condition (Nabokov's original vs. its manipulated version vs. control condition) as the fixed factor. As covariates, gender, age, and reading frequency were used. The MANOVA yielded a significant effect for eternal love, $F(2, 44) = 3.79$, $p < .05$, $MSE = 1.26$. Simple planned contrasts revealed a significant difference at the .05 level between control group scores ($M = 5.07$, $SD = 1.09$) and those for the Nabokov readers ($M = 5.97$, $SD = .71$). No significant difference was found when comparing control group participants and readers of the manipulated version of the poem ($M = 5.05$, $SD = 1.52$). None of the covariates affected the scores.

The results for the second factor, power of love, are marginally significant, $F(2, 44) = 2.64$, $p = .084$, $MSE = 1.55$, with significantly higher scores for the Nabokov readers ($M = 6.00$, $SD = .73$) as compared to the control group ($M = 5.05$, $SD = 1.40$), and no significant difference between the readers of the manipulated version ($M = 5.24$, $SD = 1.42$) and the control group.

Discussion

The manipulation of foregrounding was responsible for the interaction effect found on depth of appreciation. As to the nature of this effect for this particular text, results show that it was enjoyment rather than perceived literariness or its perceived interest for others. The interaction can probably not be interpreted as a mere side effect of increased text comprehension. It seems more likely that depth of appreciation is an indication of aesthetic feelings that emerged after the second reading of the text. Also, readers seem to have been aware of the emergent effects. The Nabokov group reported having seen more aspects in the poem after second reading and expected to see even more after a third reading. But for them, this was unrelated to the discovery of ambiguity or extra interpretation levels.

This may account for the fact that the direction of the effect was not as predicted. It was assumed that the poem's third level of interpretation (the fleeting nature of feelings of romantic love) would result in lower scores on eternal love as compared to control group scores. It may be argued that the Nabokov readers remained with the second interpretation level and did not recognize the third. They might have noticed aspects (e.g., the circular structure of the poem) that foreground eternal love, but missed the transitory aspects (e.g., the symbolic value of *river* and *swift*) or interpreted them differently. Readers of the manipulation never got any further than the first, as there was no second, let alone a third, level.

GENERAL DISCUSSION

Textual features seem to cause emergent literary effects. Earlier, it was shown that narrator ambiguity and complexity produce such effects (Dixon et al., 1993; Hakemulder et al., 2003). Here, it was shown that a quality typical for literary texts—foregrounding—does so, too. Results of Experiment 1 suggest that foregrounding in the Rushdie text is responsible for emergent effects (perceived literary quality, enjoyment, and readers' interest in the rest of the text). In case of the Nabokov text, foregrounding was found to be responsible for increases in enjoyment. Readers seem aware of these emergent effects. In Experiment 2, foregrounding caused readers to indicate that they had enjoyed rereading the poem, that they became aware of aspects in the poem they had not seen the first time, and that they expected to discover even more after reading the text once more. Clearly, literary reading experiences emerge over time (cf. Dixon et al., 1993), and they can be brought about by foregrounding.

The results contradict suggestions that just any text can generate literary reading experiences. It may be that participants' responses were guided by conventions (more in particular Schmidt's, 1980, 1982, aesthetic and polyvalence convention). The studies presented here have shown, however, that literary text qualities are probably a condition for triggering such responses. Also, the design of the studies warrants the conclusion that author's or publisher's status did not play a role in the differences generated by the foregrounding manipulation.

This does not rule out the possibility that literary reading experiences are the result of an interaction between text variables and reader variables (such as literary socialization). In Dixon et al. (1993), it was found that literary effects may depend on reported reading frequency. Similarly, comparing the results of the pilot study and Experiment 1, it may be suggested that depth of appreciation depends on the degree to which readers are trained in analyzing literary texts. However, the results of Experiment 2 do not support this conclusion, for reported reading frequency did not affect depth of appreciation. The question remains why results have been unclear about the role of this factor. In some of the studies that were discussed, literary effects depended on reader variables, whereas in other studies, they did not. In future research, it may be considered to use more refined measures assessing reading habits, genre preferences, attitudes toward literature, and so on. In addition, it may be helpful to clarify, on a conceptual level, the exact text variables that are manipulated. What precisely is the relation between narrator ambiguity, complexity, the forms of foregrounding that were manipulated in the studies presented here, and those that were measured in the designs of van Peer (1986b) and Miall and Kuiken (1994)? Maybe this could help explaining the interaction between reading frequency and text variables.

The results of Experiments 1 and 2 indicate that there may be a link between foregrounding and the effect the text has on readers' awareness of things in the world outside the text (i.e., the immigrant experience and the concept of love). These findings were interpreted as renewed awareness (cf. Shklovsky, 1965). The direction of the effect was as expected for the Rusdhie text, whereas it was not for the Nabokov text. This discrepancy is probably due to differences between the texts. The intention of the irony in Rushdie's text is hard to ignore. Even though the Nabokov poem seems much easier to understand, its deeper nuances are subtler and harder to grasp than that of the Rushdie text, even after two readings. Conceivably, for the effects to take the predicted direction, more reflection and interpretation was required. As mentioned before, readers did not report to have recognized any ambiguity or deeper layers of interpretation in the text, although they had a feeling that there was more to be discovered than they had after second reading.

It must be emphasized that it is surprising that, even with short texts as those used in this study (around 600 words in Experiment 1 and a mere 64 in Experiment 2, and relatively small participant numbers), significant effects on perception were found. It may be that the rereading procedure itself added to the effect, and, therefore, it may be precarious to generalizing these findings to all reading situations. On the other hand, in many naturally occurring situations, literary texts are studied and reflected on, and it may be that the effects of such close readings are even stronger than those obtained here through a simple rereading procedure.

A challenge for future research will be to respond to the concerns raised by the institutional approach to literature (cf. Verdaasdonk, 1983). One possibility to do so would be to include author status in research designs. In these experiments, participants were kept unaware of the name of the authors (and no one guessed it was Rushdie or Nabokov). This was done to avoid having the status of the author interfere in the reading experience. It may be that a higher status of the author entices readers to a different mode of processing. Assuming the text is written by a renowned author (as opposed to, e.g., by the experimenter or a debut author who publishes exclusively on his or her own Web site), they may read more carefully, paying more attention to the surface structure of the text, and being more prone to expect it to reveal deeper insights. This may result in a greater depth of appreciation and stronger effects on perception. It would be exciting to find out, in future studies, whether this would eliminate the effects of text qualities, as some theorists would predict.

Furthermore, future research should focus on enhancing control over participants' text processing. In the studies presented here, the rereading method was used to stimulate a more careful reading of the text. It was assumed that, when participants were asked to read the text a second time, they took the opportunity to reflex more on its hidden meaning and locate those text aspects that may help them to interpret the text. However, with the research design presented here, it is unclear what participants exactly did during second reading. Nor is it clear whether their interpretation after the second reading really differed from that after the first. Future on-line research should remedy this problem. To increase control, it may be considered to instruct participants to produce an interpretation of the text and compare the effects with participants that are given another reading instruction.

The advantages of the method of the rereading paradigm lie in the fact that it allows itself for systematic research of text features causing literary reading experiences. By means of manipulation of isolated text variables, it may be examined whether depth of appreciation is affected by them. Moreover, it seems that a similar approach may be applied to other art forms. It may be that the depth of appreciation phenomenon also occurs in responses to film and music. Also, here one may attempt to establish, through text manipulation, which intrinsic qualities are responsible for differences in responses. It may be argued that the resulting insights could reveal what the essence of art is, and what it does to people.

ACKNOWLEDGMENTS

Part of the research this article is based on (the pilot study and Experiment 1) was financed by *The Multicultural and Multiform Society*, a national project of The Netherlands Organization for Scientific Research. I thank Willie van Peer and Nadia Kaddioui for their comments on an earlier version of this article. For suggesting the Nabokov text and its reading, thanks to colleagues at the Department of Literary Studies, Utrecht University. Also thanks to Peter Dixon and Marissa Bortolussi for sharing the full questionnaire of their 1993 research.

REFERENCES

Allen, M., & Preiss, R. W. (1997). Comparing the persuasiveness of narrative and statistical evidence using meta-analysis. *Communication Research Report, 14,* 125–131.

Ashby, M. S., & Wittmaier, B. C. (1978). Attitude changes in children after exposure to stories about women in traditional or nontraditional occupations. *Journal of Educational Psychology, 70,* 945–949.

Barclay, L. K. (1974). The emergence of vocational expectations in preschool children. *Journal of Vocational Behavior, 4,* 1–14.

Berg-Cross, L., & Berg-Cross, G. (1978). Listening to stories may change children's social attitudes. *The Reading Teacher, 32,* 659–663.

Biskin, D. S., & Hoskisson, K. (1977). An experimental test of the effects of structured discussions of moral dilemmas found in children's literature on moral reasoning. *The Elementary School Journal, 78,* 407–416.

Booth, W. (1988). *The company we keep: An ethics of fiction.* Berkeley: University of California Press.

Bourdieu, P. (1984). *Distinction.* London: Routledge & Kegan Paul.

Bourg, T., Risden, K., Thompson, S., & Davis, E. C. (1993). The effects of an empathy-building strategy on 6th graders' causal inferencing in narrative text comprehension. *Poetics, 22,* 117–133.

Brisbin, C. D. (1971). *An experimental application of the galvanic skin response to the measurement of the effects of literature on attitudes on fifth grade students toward blacks.* Unpublished doctoral dissertation, Wayne State University, Detroit, Michigan.

Dixon, P., Bortolussi, M., Twilley, L. C., & Leung, A. (1993). Literary processing and interpretation: Toward empirical foundations. *Poetics, 22,* 5–33.

Egan, K. (1988). *Teaching as storytelling.* London: Routledge.

Erlich, V. (1980). *Russian formalism: History–doctrine.* The Hague, The Netherlands: Mouton.

Fish, S. (1980). *Is there a text in this class? The authority of interpretive communities.* Cambridge, MA: Harvard University Press.

Flerx, V. C., Fidler, D. S., & Rogers, R. W. (1976). Sex role stereotypes: Developmental aspects and early intervention. *Child Development, 47*, 998–1007.

Gallagher, W. J. (1978). *Implementation of a Kohlbergian value development curriculum in high school literature.* Unpublished doctoral dissertation, Fordham University, New York.

Gardner, J. (1978). *On moral fiction.* Chicago: HarperCollins.

Garrod, A. C. (1982). *A developmental approach to the teaching of literature: A context for moral and ego growth in adolescents.* Unpublished doctoral dissertation, Harvard University, Cambridge, MA.

Geiger, K. F. (1975). Jugendliche lesen 'Landser'-Hefte: Hinweise auf Lektürefunktionen und-wirkungen [Jung people read 'Landser' booklets: Evidence for the function and effect of reading]. In G. Grimm (Ed.), *Literatur und Leser: Theorien und Modelle zur Rezeption literarischer Werke* (pp. 324–341). Stuttgart, Germany: Reclam.

Hakemulder, J. (2000). *The moral laboratory: Experiments examining the effects of reading literature on social perception and moral self-knowledge.* Amsterdam: Benjamins.

Hakemulder, J. (2001). How to make *alle Menschen Brüder*: Literature in a multicultural and multiform society. In D. Schram & G. Steen (Eds.), *The psychology and sociology of literature* (pp. 225–242). Amsterdam: Benjamins.

Hakemulder, J., van Peer, W., & Zyngier, S. (2003). *Rereading complex texts.* Unpublished manuscript.

Hermans, M., & Hakemulder, J. (2003). *Immigrant literature in the classroom.* Unpublished manuscript.

Herrnstein Smith, B. (1988). *Contingencies of value: Alternative perspectives for critical theory.* Cambridge, MA: Harvard University Press.

Horace. (1986). On the art of poetry. In T. S. Dorsch (Ed.), *Classical literary criticism* (pp. 77–96). Harmondsworth, England: Penguin.

Iser, W. (1970). *Die Appellstruktur der Texte: Unbestimmtheit als Wirkungsbedingung literarisher Prosa* [The appeal structure of the text: Indeterminateness as a condition for the effect of literary prose]. Konstanz, Germany: Universitäts Verlag.

Jackson, E. P. (1944). Effect of reading upon attitudes toward the Negro race. *Library Quarterly, 14*, 47–54.

Jakobson, R. (1960). Linguistics and poetics. In T. A. Sebeok (Ed.), *Style in language* (pp. 350–358). Cambridge, MA: MIT Press.

Johnson, E. M. W. (1990). *Literary interpretation and moral reasoning in patterns of transescent students in selected middle schools.* Unpublished doctoral dissertation, Georgia State University, Atlanta.

Justice, M. C. (1989). *The effects of literature instruction with an emphasis on Kohlberg's moral development stages on secondary students' moral reasoning abilities.* Unpublished doctoral dissertation, East Texas State University, Marshall.

Keefe, D. R. (1975). *A comparison of the effect of teacher and student led discussions of short stories and case accounts on the moral reasoning of adolescents using the Kohlberg model.* Unpublished doctoral dissertation, University of Illinois, Urbana-Champaign.

Kinnard, F. H. (1986). *The effects of two young adult novels on the cognitive development of moral reasoning.* Unpublished doctoral dissertation, Vanderbilt University, Nashville, Tennessee.

Kraaykamp, G. (1993). *Over lezen gesproken: Een studie naar sociale differentiatie in leesgedrag* [Speaking of reading: A study on social differentiation in reading behavior]. Amsterdam: Thesis Publishers.

Litcher, J. H., & Johnson, D. W. (1969). Changes in attitudes toward Negroes of white elementary school students after use of multiethnic readers. *Journal of Educational Psychology, 60*, 148–152.

McArthur, L. Z., & Eisen, S. V. (1976). Achievements of male and female storybook characters as determinants of achievement behavior by boys and girls. *Journal of Personality and Social Psychology, 33*, 467–473.

Miall, D. S., & Kuiken, D. (1994). Foregrounding, defamiliarization, and affect: Response to literary stories. *Poetics, 22*, 389–407.

Mukarovsky, J. (1964). Standard language and poetic language. In P. L. Garvin (Ed.), *A Prague school reader on esthetics, literary structure, and style* (pp. 17–30). Washington, DC: Georgetown University Press.

Nabokov, V. (1996). The old bridge. In P. Verstegen (Ed.), *Natuur zal kunst nooit blijvend evenaren: De Westeuropese poëzie in honderd gedichten* [Nature will never match art permanently: West-European poetry in hundred poems] (p. 114). Amsterdam: Ooievaar.

Nussbaum, M. C. (1991). The literary imagination in public life. *New Literary History, 22,* 877–910.

Palmer, F. (1992). *Literature and moral understanding: A philosophical essay on ethics, aesthetics, education, and culture.* Oxford, England: Clarendon.

Reinard, J. (1988). The empirical study of the persuasive effects of evidence: The status after fifty years of research. *Human Communication Research, 15,* 3–59.

Rorty, R. (1989). *Contingency, irony, and solidarity.* Cambridge, England: Cambridge University Press.

Rushdie, S. (1988). *The Satanic verses.* New York: Viking.

Rushdie, S. (1991). *Imaginary homelands: Essays and criticism 1981–1991.* London: Granta Books.

Schmidt, S. J. (1980 & 1982). *Grundriss der empirische Literaturwissenschaft* [Basis for the empirical study of literature]. Braunschweig, Germany: Vieweg & Sohn.

Schram, D., & Geljon, C. (1988). Effecten van affectieve en cognitieve lesmethoden op de receptie van verhalen over de Tweede Wereldoorlog [Effects of affective and cognitive didactic methods on response to World War II stories]. *Spiegel, 6,* 31–54.

Shelley, P. B. (1977). A defence of poetry, or remarks suggested by an essay entitled "The four ages of poetry." In D. H. Reiman & S. B. Powers (Eds.), *Shelley's poetry and prose: Authorative texts, criticism* (pp. 478–508). New York: Norton.

Shklovsky, V. (1965). Art as technique. In L. T. Lemon & M. J. Reis (Eds. & Trans.), *Russian formalist criticism: Four essays* (pp. 3–24). Lincoln: University of Nebraska Press.

Steiner, G. (1989). *Real presences: Is there anything in what we say?* London: Faber & Faber.

Stempel, W. (Ed.). (1972). *Texte der russische Formalisten II* [Russian formalists texts II]. München, Germany: Fink.

Tauran, R. H. (1967). *The influences of reading on the attitudes of third graders toward Eskimos.* Unpublished dissertation, University of Maryland, College Park.

van Peer, W. (1986a). Pulp and purpose: Stylistic analysis as an aid to a theory of texts. In T. D'Haen (Ed.), *Linguistics and the study of literature* (pp. 268–286). Amsterdam: Rodopi.

van Peer, W. (1986b). *Stylistics and psychology: Investigations of foregrounding.* London: Croom Helm.

van Rees, K., Vermunt, J., & Verboord, M. (1999). Cultural classification under discussion: Latent class analysis of highbrow and lowbrow reading. *Poetics, 26,* 349–365.

Verdaasdonk, H. (1983). Social and economic factors in the attribution of literary quality. *Poetics, 12,* 383–395.

Zola, E. (1968). Le roman expérimental [The experimental novel]. In H. Mitterand (Ed.), *Oeuvres complètes* (Vol. 10, pp. 1173–1401). Paris: Cercle du Livre Précieux.

Zucaro, B. J. (1972). *The use of bibliotherapy among sixth graders to affect attitude change toward American Negroes.* Unpublished dissertation, Temple University, Philadelphia.

DISCOURSE PROCESSES, *38*(2), 219–246

Reality-Based Genre Preferences Do Not Direct Personal Involvement

Elly A. Konijn
Department of Communication Science
Free University, Amsterdam, The Netherlands

Johan F. Hoorn
Department of Computer Science
Free University, Amsterdam, The Netherlands

Although it seems plausible that people who prefer a particular genre would appreciate characters from that category more than those from other genres, this appears not to be the case. We devised a parsimonious reality-based genre taxonomy that differentiates nonfiction, realism, fantasy, and humor. In Study 1, evidence from film viewers' genre preferences prompted slight adjustments in that taxonomy. In Study 2, however, we found that their reality-based genre preferences did not predict personal involvement with, distance from, or liking for the protagonist in the preferred genre. Instead, the represented and, particularly, the perceived realism of the character did affect personal involvement, but irrespective of genre preferences. We discuss the implications of these results for the rationale behind a genre typology and for engaging with fictional characters to explain personal involvement and character appreciation, especially in motion pictures.

Distinguishing genres in the cultural domain is an example of grouping behavior. People group things together for data reduction, so that they can judge a few categories instead of many instances. Whether valid, the function of such heuristics is that one can infer that "what applies to the group also applies to its members." Extending this heuristic to genres, preferences can be justified, such as "If you like sci-fi, you will like Buck Rogers" (Nowlan, 1928). However, people group things

---

Correspondence and requests for reprints should be sent to Elly A. Konijn, Free University, Department of Communication Science, Faculty of Social Sciences, De Boelelaan 1081-c, 1081 HV Amsterdam, The Netherlands. E-mail: ea.konijn@fsw.vu.nl

together with a goal in mind. If someone collects romantic poetry, Coleridge is included and De Ronsard is excluded. If someone collects books for high status, Einstein (science) stands side by side with Rembrandt (art) and the Bible (religion). Therefore, the history of classifying cultural products has left us with a great diversity of taxonomies, because these were set up with quite different criteria in mind (see Steen, 1999).

Traditional genre classifications often are liable to the "inherent quality fallacy," claiming that a work belongs to a group because of (text) immanent properties without accounting for the goals of the human classifier. Nowadays, bookshops and other media distributors use an amalgamation of types and classes, which, from a scientific point of view, offer little systematic discrimination among readers' or viewers' perceptions (Bordwell, 1989, p. 147). It should be admitted, then, that genre taxonomies shift when people change their objectives in the examination of cultural products (see Chandler, 2000, for nice examples in "The Problem of Definition"). Genre discussions are pointless if the goal of a classification remains implicit. In line with Freedman and Medway (1994, pp. 1–20) and Livingstone (1990, p. 155), classifications are vulnerable to values, norms, worldviews, and ideologies, which may differ from time to time and from culture to culture. Psychological approaches to genre often focus on typicality or similarity as the unifying concept (e.g., Martindale, 1996; Piters & Stokmans, 2000) or study the affective effects of certain genres (e.g., Gunter & Furham, 1984; Zillmann, 1996). Here, we like to limit the criteria by which similarity is judged, propose a reality-based conception of genre preferences, and study the effects of genre preferences on personal involvement.

If classifications depend on a worldview (Freedman & Medway, 1994), then, despite their diversity, genre taxonomies may in general have two aspects: on the product side, the represented reality and, on the receiver's side, the perceived realism of that represented reality. These two aspects of genre taxonomies do not necessarily correspond, although it is generally assumed that genre sets the boundaries for how a work should be interpreted. For example, it is unreasonable to disapprove of talking animals in fables, because the very genre depends on this "unrealistic" combination of character attributes. Hence, *represented reality* is the degree to which a product portrays realistic and unrealistic features (a characteristic of the stimulus), and *perceived realism* is the degree to which the receiver judges that reality is reflected in a media product. In this article, we attempt to develop a genre classification founded on the degree of represented reality, as a product feature. This we call the *reality-based genres*: genres that are grouped in a product analysis according to their degrees of presumed represented reality. We empirically validate the reality-based genre taxonomy from a receiver's perspective by means of what we call the *reality-based genre preferences*: empirically assessed clusters of conventional-genre preferences of receivers that correspond with reality-based genres. In line with Durkin (1985), Livingstone (1989), and Miall and Kuiken

(1998, 1999), we demonstrate that the analyses of product features should be complemented by studies of viewers' perceptions and experiences.

Furthermore, we investigate whether our reality-based genre taxonomy can predict the receiver's experience of personal involvement with the main character of a work. In our view, involvement includes identification and empathy, among other affective states, and is a central concept in studying the reader's/viewer's experiences and liking of a character (Hoorn & Konijn, 2003; Konijn, 1999; Oatley, 1994, 1999; Raney & Bryant, 2002; Tan, 1996; Zillmann, 1996, p. 209). The experience of involvement is important to motivate active participation in discussions of, for example, the morality of a character (e.g., Vorderer, 2000, p. 68); to encourage the formation of opinions about what could be true in real life; and to foster experimentation with sympathy and antipathy toward dissimilar others. We examine whether preference for a genre, as defined by its style of representing reality, positively affects involvement with the protagonist.

REALITY-BASED GENRE TAXONOMY

From the work of Fitch, Huston, and Wright (1993), one can deduce that genre taxonomies provide schemata that structure and guide media experiences. Oatley (1994) even posited that there is a genre for each emotional theme, such as "romances for feeling happy," "thrillers for feeling anxious," and "weepies for sadness" (p. 69). Although our studies focus on film classification and engagement with movie characters, we assume that empirical work in literary studies are also relevant to our aims. Therefore, we consulted studies of visual as well as textual media to arrive at a genre taxonomy that may cover both fields.

At a time in which broadcasted information is contaminated with war propaganda and commercial persuasion, in which teachers become mediated persons on the Internet, and in which surgeons tele-operate real-life patients via their virtual counterparts, it is worthwhile to study whether people perceive mediated information as realistic or unrealistic (cf. Chandler, 2000; Gerbner, Gross, Morgan, & Signorielli, 1994). In doing so, it is evident that the level of represented reality and perceived realism in media productions have particular importance (cf. information reality in Shapiro & McDonald, 1992). Hoorn, Konijn, and Van der Veer (2003) argued that cultural products simultaneously have realistic and unrealistic aspects. For example, documentaries, news items, and biopics are primarily focused on information that is checked for its reality status and that is socially accepted as "factual." In contrast, fantasy games, tabloid articles, and hagiologies are primarily fostered by the imagination of their creators, without much concern about an accurate rendering of what is socially accepted as "reality." However, between these extremes, and sometimes even within, there is no strict divide. Highly respected newspapers still have a political color, and tabloids sometimes have a scoop that is picked up and elaborated by the journalistic establishment. News items broadcasted through multimedia have, apart from using text and image, even more potential to manipulate the representation of reality by editing sound, motion, and sometimes haptic information, usually under the assumption that receivers experience more "presence," "immersion," or parasocial interaction (Horton & Wohl, 1956/1986) when more sensory channels are activated (Blascovich, Loomis, Beall, Swinth, Hoyt, & Bailenson, 2002; Monk & Gale, 2002). Mallon (2002) stated

> At a time when important filmmakers and serious novelists are turning to historical subjects with unusual frequency, their audiences find themselves left to ponder and preserve the distinctions between facts and fabrications.

In general, mixes of realistic and unrealistic features are characteristic of the stories and characters that are conveyed to the receiver, and whether the realistic or unrealistic side dominates often depends on the sender's objective. In certain cases, genre boundaries may be deliberately made uncertain (e.g., in propaganda), and new mixes of realistic and unrealistic features may be developed (e.g., in infotainment) when this is beneficial to the sender.

As long as artists, writers, and filmmakers like to mix genres so that the number of hybrids increases, the number of genre labels will increase as well (Nichols, 1991). Considering product features, as most conventional approaches do (cf. Book Nuts Reading Club, 2003), cultural products group together under a miscellany of labels (e.g., *docudrama, action-comedy,* and *fake-documentary*). However, because genre boundaries and genre transgressions seem to be associated with the (sometimes blurred) boundaries between fact and fabrication, we hypothesize that grouping products on a criterion of reality representation will lead to a more parsimonious taxonomy that, moreover, makes sense to the receiver's perception of the work.

In the following, we attempt to group conventional genres according to their style of representing reality. That is, within a given genre, a situation, event, or character can be represented as more realistic (following the laws of nature and the practices of daily life) or more unrealistic (following magical, mythical, or fantastic ideas). The result of our attempt is presented in Table 1 and is elaborated following. In compiling a preliminary taxonomy of genres, we used the extant literature in describing salient features of the conventional genres such that they could be grouped according to their degree of represented reality and analyzed as a feature of the product. The product features that we used to decide whether a conventional genre belonged to one or the other reality-based genre in our taxonomy are the represented degrees of reality in the filmic situation, event, and character. In Table 1, the result of this product analysis is given in columns 3 through 6 and is described next. Furthermore, in Study 1, we provide evidence for the grouping criterion of represented reality by confronting our taxonomy with viewers' judgments.

TABLE 1
Reality-Based Genre Taxonomy Derived From Literature on Reality Representations

Reality Representation: Realistic Fiction–Unrealistic Fiction	Product Type/ Conventional Labels	Situation/ Event	Focal Point	Actions	Information Type
Reality registration	Nonfiction (e.g., documentary, news, science)	Direct observation of daily life	Persons	Natural	Information reality
Reality simulation	Realism (e.g., psychological, drama, realism, romance, virtual reality)	As if daily life affairs	Impersonated characters	Performed (staged, acting)	Social and interpersonal reality
Marvels	Fantasy (e.g., thriller, sci-fi, horror, action, myth)	Extraordinary (not daily life) affairs	Detached characters	Faked (invented, fabled)	Possible worlds
Absurdism	Humor (e.g., comedy, cartoons)	Deviation and disruption of daily life	Performers	Illogical	Reflective

Note. This taxonomy is hypothetical. The first and second columns are subjected to the empirical Study 1.

REALITY REGISTRATION

Documentaries and journalism (Table 1, row 1) usually concentrate on a realistic style of representation, depicting daily life as directly and truly as possible (row 1, column 3), focusing on real persons (column 4), and presenting actions as natural and likely to occur (column 5; Bazin, 1962; Nichols, 1991). Here, the director, framing, and camera work can deliberately create a realistic style of representation. For example, reality judgments of TV events are attached to certain (formal) cuing features of the genre, such as when TV newsreaders face the camera (suggesting objective representation), whereas actors-as-characters usually do not (Davies, 1997, pp. 6, 35, 46). Also, in news and documentaries, cuts, focal plane, and topic selection actually mismatch our natural modes of stimulus perception (cf. "TV forms" in Fitch et al., 1993). In other words, this genre registers facts, but these registrations are never without fabrications (cf. Mallon, 2002). Accordingly, documentaries may be conceived as a realistic genre of *fiction* (cf. Hoorn et al., 2003), although the conventional label for such productions is *nonfiction* (column 2). Such media presentations have a high degree of information reality (column 6)—that is, the extent to which a media presentation provides information about reality (Shapiro & McDonald, 1992).

Reality Simulation

Certain documentary makers increase the number of unrealistic features by reconstructing a crime site, allowing actors to replay an emotional scene, and trying to evoke suspense with sinister music and fast montage (e.g., BBC1's *Crimewatch UK*). Together with reality soaps, such docudramas form the border with what usually is called *realism* (Table 1, row 2, column 2; Kracauer, 1960), but what we call *reality simulation* (row 2, column 1). What soap operas, psychodramas, or Zola's social realism have in common with virtual reality (VR) and computer simulations is that they offer an artificial replication, a realistic imitation, or a model of reality rather than a direct registration (Oatley, 1999). Situations and events from daily life are designed and acted out in a lifelike manner, but the make-believe is stronger than in documentaries (column 3). Romantic motion pictures can also be viewed as realistic simulations of interpersonal relationships (Schatz, 1981). The characters are played by actors who, in a sense, impersonate an imagined person (column 4). Prominent examples of this approach are found in method acting, where actors are asked to "become" the character they play and where "truthful emotions" are expected (Konijn, 2000). Actions are performed, not registered, but in a truthful manner; it should be possible to meet such people and encounter such situations in real life (column 5; Horton & Wohl, 1956/1986; Livingstone, 1989). Due to the focus on impersonated characters, what readers/viewers can learn from this kind of realistic production is directed toward social and interpersonal authenticity (column 6) or what is called *social reality construction* (Gerbner et al., 1994) and *exemplar accessibility* (Zillmann, 2002).

Marvels

The transition from realistic to unrealistic representation is established when situations and events surpass daily life affairs (Table 1, row 3, column 3; Tan, 1996, p. 51). A label that comes to mind is *fantasy* (row 3, column 2), but we find this term too restricted to sorcery, fairy tales, and the supernatural (see Grodal, 2000, pp. 99–100), such as the Hobbit or Harry Potter. Although adventures and action are often highly fantastic, they are not necessarily magical as the term *fantasy* connotes. The "marvel" in such genres is in opening up worlds ordinary people are unlikely to enter. Hanging from a cliff as target practice for a gunman in a helicopter, then falling into a tree that pushes its branches through his limbs, after which John Rambo kills everyone who comes in his way, is not the life of an average GI Joe. Sci-fi and horror productions explore galaxies and psychic dimensions one can only dream of. In other words, the actions are faked (cf. special effects) and often performed by a stunt (wo)man, simulated in a studio or by computers (column 5). In evading real-life situations and people, then, marvels present more detached characters (column 4; Tan, 1996, p. 175). Marvel heroes are invincible, untouchable, and do not suffer from human inconveniences, such as going to the toilet or having to bathe the children. Marvels satisfy curiosity about the possibilities of living under unusual conditions (e.g., Rambo), discovering unique worlds (e.g., Star Trek), and having higher powers and senses (e.g., Superman, The Sentinel; column 6).

Absurdism

Because of their dazzling effects, high technical performance, and extreme situations, it is hard to suppress a smile while perceiving marvels. To a large extent, the fun is in the exaggeration. What traditionally is labeled *humor* (Table 1, row 4, column 2; Heil, 2002; McGhee & Goldstein, 1983; Zubarev, 1999) exploits this experience even more extensively. Overstatement (e.g., in comedy) and understatement (e.g., in irony) are two styles of representing the world that are much appreciated by humorists. Cartoon and animation figures are stretched to express speed or squeezed together to express a sudden stop. The banana peel joke as well as the subtle satire of Goethe's *Faust* (part I) have in common that fixed patterns of behavior (e.g., walking, defying the devil) are deautomated (cf. Ruch, 1993). Jokes draw on deviation from convention and disruption of daily life (e.g., falling down, sympathy for the devil) by making reality larger than life or by intending the opposite of what was expressed. Humoristic products focus on (exploring the psyche of) the performer (cf. stand-up comedians, Woody Allen movies; column 4) rather than exploring the deeper feelings of an impersonated character or the epic transactions of an invulnerable hero. Whether understated or overstated, the actions comedians perform are absurd or illogical, given the situations and events with which they have to deal (column 5). They often provide pointed commentaries about social conventions and cultural rules.

Now that we have analyzed the represented reality in specific product features of conventional genres to discern the categories in our presumed taxonomy, we analyze its potential from the receiver's perspective. One of the central issues from a reader's/viewer's perspective is getting involved (Tan, 1996; Vorderer, 2000; Zillmann, 1994). Therefore, what are the implications of a presumed reality-based genre taxonomy for the personal involvement of the receiver?

INVOLVEMENT

To enhance involvement, reality-mimicking genres such as soap operas, (fake) documentaries, docudrama, and reality TV try to trick observers into believing that what they see really has happened. However, TV reality is different from real-world reality (Davies, 1997, p. 33). Movies merely have a degree of realism, reflecting a number of realistic features (p. 45) in contrast to a number of unrealistic features. For each feature, genre or style conventions form the parameters for the right degree of realistic and unrealistic appearances. In the classic conception (from Aristotle to method acting), it is assumed that an increase in the number of realistic features evokes stronger involvement in the receiver.

Smith (1995, p. 94) stated that the strongest provoker of involvement, the "identification figure," is the protagonist of a work (see also Vorderer, 2000, p. 68). Zubarev (1999) saw a direct link between the protagonist and genre attribution. She stated that genre is determined by the protagonists' potential to affect "the future development of their environment." A tragic hero, for instance, has a large potential to change a situation (but makes mistakes), whereas a comedy character has low potential to do so: "any interpreter, including the artist ... gives weight to the protagonist ... , in defining the genre of a literary work." A tragedy is heartbreaking because the vicissitudes and mindstate of the hero are. A comedy is funny because the situations and the character's responses to them are judged scabrous. Livingstone (1989) added that characters are essential to understanding the viewer's involvement with soap operas and that character representation is important to framing the narrative's moral stance.

Genres are sometimes assumed to reflect a worldview (Freedman & Medway, 1994, pp. 1–20; Livingstone, 1990, p. 155), and, by implication, characters may help to establish and reflect those worldviews. Worldviews in media portrayals become visible in how reality is represented or, as Shapiro and McDonald (1992) called it, in the "information reality" of a media product. Characters usually carry the information of a plot, story, or narrative and are important in evoking certain degrees of involvement (e.g., Hoffner & Cantor, 1991; Livingstone, 1989; Smith, 1995, p. 94; Vorderer, 2000, p. 68). Through their characters, then, genres invite involvement in the bearers of certain worldviews.

Furthermore, popular opinion as well as certain studies in mass media effects (e.g., Atkin, 1983; Berkowitz & Alioto, 1973) would have it that more realistic genres evoke more personal involvement with the protagonist and thus more appreciation. The popularity of certain genres, such as reality TV, reality soaps, and stories based on facts, and the status of certain dramatic styles, such as method acting, seem to underscore that position. Therefore, our focus in Study 2 is whether genres that are considered realistic lead to increased personal involvement with the protagonist compared with protagonists of genres that are considered unrealistic. However, first we have to test the empirical validity of our presumed reality-based genre taxonomy.

STUDY 1

The aim of Study 1 was to examine whether the reality-based genre taxonomy presented in Table 1, which stretches from reality registration through reality simulation to marvels and absurdity, fits with readers'/viewers' perspectives. There are several ways to arrive at such a test. Instead of directly asking the respondents how they classify specific genre labels, we opted for an indirect measure, which may be more reliable in measuring complex constructs (Dillman, 1979; Oosterveld, 1996). This indirect measure consisted of asking the respondents about their individual preferences for particular (conventional) genres, instead of asking them to categorize the genre.

Furthermore, the choice of genre preferences also has a theoretical basis to the extent that indicating preference for a genre may reflect preference for a certain worldview (Freedman & Medway, 1994; Livingstone, 1990). *Genre preferences* may thus be seen as the indirect reflection of grouping behavior on a criterion of reality representation. Therefore, it seems reasonable to expect that genre preferences that reflect more realistic compared to more unrealistic worldviews may group together. If the assumption that genres reflect certain worldviews is correct, preferences for particular genres should be closely related to the degree of represented reality. In other words, we hypothesize that the degree and style of representing reality within a given genre will underlie genre preferences. Thus, it should be possible to reliably group the respondents' preferences for conventional genres according to the reality-based taxonomy that was proposed in Table 1. A hierarchical cluster analysis (HCA) of the respondents' preferences for conventional film genres, then, should correspond to the reality-based genre taxonomy in Table 1.

Method

Participants.   A diverse sample of undergraduate students participated in this experiment for payment, 312 in total (136 men, 175 women; M age 22.4, $SD = 5.74$). They reported backgrounds in various disciplines. The participants in Study 1 were the same as in Study 2.

Measurements.   From the literature on film genres (e.g., Bordwell, 1989; Bordwell, Staiger, & Thompson, 1985; Chandler, 2000; Dirks, 2002) and surveys on film viewing, we compiled a number of common and representative genre labels for the four reality-based genre categories of Table 1. We presented 12 questions concerning genre preferences, in random order, in a paper–pencil questionnaire to the respondents in this study. The first reality-based genre category, *reality registration* (see Table 1), was exemplified by the item "documentary." Items for the second reality-based genre category, *reality simulation*, were "realistic films," "psychological films," "drama," and "romance." The items "action films," "sci-fi," "horror," and "thriller" represented the third reality-based genre category, *marvels.* The fourth, *absurdism*, was reflected by the items "comedy/humor" and "cartoons/animation films." An item called "other" was included so that participants could write down a preferred genre that was not listed. Respondents were asked to indicate their preferences by checking each conventional genre label with yes or no. Furthermore, the questionnaire contained items related to Study 2 (such as involvement, distance, and appreciation—see following) and demographic variables, such as gender and age.

Results and Discussion

Participants by genre.   In Table 2, the conventional-genre preferences of men are compared with those of women. Five out of 12 genre items show differences between the sexes of more than 10%. For example, 60% of women preferred drama, as opposed to 29% of men viewers. In general, women preferred drama, romantic, and realistic films more than men, who preferred action and horror (cf. Cohen & Weimann, 2000). However, these differences are not critical in this analysis of clustering preferences to warrant separate analyses of the sexes. Furthermore, as is shown in Study 2, gender as a covariate appeared to be insignificant to predict involvement.

Clustering of genre preferences.   An HCA was performed over the questionnaire answers that related to genre preferences. Note that the HCA was used to

TABLE 2
Conventional-Genre Preferences × Sex

Conventional-Genre Preference: Yes	Men		Women	
	Count	%	Count	%
Thriller	86	63.2	109	62.3
Documentary	61	44.9	75	42.9
Comedy	90	66.2	107	61.1
Drama	40	**29.4**	106	**60.6**
Action	67	**49.3**	45	**25.7**
Sci-fi	43	**31.6**	24	**13.7**
Realism	60	44.1	91	52.0
Psychological	58	**42.6**	112	**64.0**
Cartoons	34	25.0	35	20.0
Romance	26	**19.1**	111	**63.4**
Horror	20	14.7	16	9.1
Other	9	6.6	15	8.6

Note. N = 312. Differences between the sexes for their genre preferences that are greater than 10% are in bold.

categorize the conventional genre labels rather than to categorize individuals. Because of the nature of the dichotomous data (yes–no), an average linkage (between groups) algorithm utilized the binary option and Jaccard's (1908) similarity ratio (Milligan & Schilling, 1985). Often, but not always, respondents left check boxes empty to give a *no-answer.* Therefore, Jaccard's method was preferred because it focuses the analysis on the *yes-answers* of the respondents.[1] Due to the binary analyses, the agglomeration schedule was hardly interpretable. We focus, then, on the dendrogram as shown in Figure 1.

The HCA provided reasonable empirical support for discerning four genre groups. However, their contents only partly match the taxonomy of Table 1. The first cluster grouped horror, cartoons, and sci-fi (bottom up in Figure 1), followed by a cluster that included action, comedy, and thriller. Finally, documentary could be distinguished as a separate cluster from romance, realistic films, psychological films, and drama. The latter two clusters coincided with realistic registration and realistic simulation, respectively (Table 1). However, the absurdism category (containing comedy and cartoons as exemplars) was spread over the first and second clusters in the analysis and thus did not seem to be a genre category of its own. Comedy, thriller, and action were grouped in the second cluster (bottom up), whereas cartoons was at best clustered with sci-fi and horror.

---

[1]The Jaccard coefficient indicates a proximation of similarity between categories and is calculated from binary data (present vs. absent). Jaccard discounts the shared absences because these are ecologically indefinite.

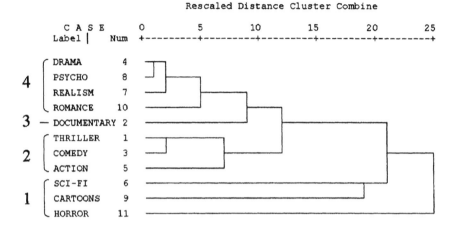

FIGURE 1   Hierarchical binary cluster analysis for respondents' genre preferences.

Results from the cluster analysis indicate that marvels as a reality-based genre in the presumed taxonomy may be divided into two groups: a weaker form, which we characterize as *believable fantasy* (comedy, action, and thrillers), and a stronger form, which we characterize as *unbelievable fantasy* (cartoons, sci-fi, and horror). Unbelievable fantasy would also probably include what traditionally is labeled *fantasy*—that is, fairy tales and supernatural stories. Some clusters appeared to be more tight (e.g., thriller, comedy, action) than other clusters (e.g., sci-fi, cartoons, horror). That horror joined the cluster relatively late is probably due to the relatively small number of respondents who checked this option as their preferred genre. In all, this suggests the necessity of replication, particularly regarding the cluster of unbelievable fantasy.

Based on the literature (e.g., Bordwell et al., 1985; Dirks, 2002) and our product analysis, we had originally distinguished humorous genres from realistic genres because humor exaggerates or understates real-world situations. However, the results presented here suggest that absurdism is distributed over believable and unbelievable fantasy, with comedy representing the more realistic and cartoons the more unrealistic variants.

Given these results, the genre taxonomy presented in Table 1 should be adjusted. We interpreted the four resulting clusters as reality-based genre preferences for reality registration, reality simulation, believable fantasy, and unbelievable fantasy. Accordingly, we adjusted the respective descriptions in Table 3. The main difference from Table 1 is in the genres of unrealistic fiction. Marvels should be divided into fantasy that is still believable, situated in worlds that possibly exist (e.g., Rambo surviving in a forest), and fantasy that is unbelievable, set in a world that is impossible (e.g., Superman on Krypton). Accordingly, characters in believable

TABLE 3
Reality-Based Genre Taxonomy Based on Clustered Genre Preferences of Respondents

Reality Representation: Realistic Fiction–Unrealistic Fiction	Product Type/ Conventional Label	Situation/ Event	Focal Point	Actions	Information Type
Reality registration	Nonfiction: documentary	Direct observation of daily life	Persons	Natural	Information reality
Reality simulation	Realism: psychological, drama, realism, romance	As if daily life affairs	Impersonated characters	Performed (staged, acting)	Social and interpersonal reality
Believable fantasy	Adventure: action, thriller, comedy	Extraordinary events in daily life	Detached characters	Faked (invented, fabled)	Possible worlds
Unbelievable fantasy	Fantasy: horror, sci-fi, cartoons	Extraordinary events, not in daily life	Caricatures	Absurd	Impossible worlds

Note. This taxonomy is based on the cluster analysis. The first column is combined into the factor reality-based genre preference (Study 2). *Marvels* (Table 1) turned out to have two subdivisions: *believable fantasy* and *unbelievable fantasy*, which is adjusted in agreement with the data of Study 1.

fantasy (e.g., comedy) may be detached persons; in unbelievable fantasy (e.g., cartoons and horror), they become caricatures. Nevertheless, a replication is wanted, and the remaining columns in Table 3 have to be empirically validated.

STUDY 2

Generating taxonomies in itself is uninteresting if the taxonomy does not clarify processes or effects in the reader/viewer (cf. Durkin, 1985; Livingstone, 1989; Miall & Kuiken, 1998). In the previous sections, we hypothesized that the presumed reality-based genres (Table 1) would affect the personal involvement with and appreciation of the protagonist in the corresponding genre. We now extend that logic to our empirically substantiated genre preferences (Table 3).

Given the results from Study 1, we were able to create four groups of respondents on the basis of their genre preferences that we interpreted as reality-based; hence, we call them *reality-based genre preferences*. In so doing, the receiver's perspective (the empirically assessed preferences) is integrated with a product feature (the presumed degree of represented reality; cf. Miall & Kuiken, 1999). A salient aspect of a genre supposedly is the protagonist (Livingstone, 1989; Zubarev, 1999). Therefore, we claim that genre preference will be reflected in preference for its protagonists. Liking a character is strongly based on involvement with the protagonist (Raney & Bryant, 2002; Zillmann, 1994; Zillmann & Cantor, 1977). We hypothesize, then, that liking a particular genre (i.e., a preference for "reality registration") evokes increased involvement with a protagonist from a corresponding genre (e.g., Gandhi) compared to protagonists of other genres (e.g., Vlad Dracul).

Thus, the effects of the reality-based genre preferences should become apparent in higher levels of appreciation for leading roles in the preferred genre than in other genres. In addition, personal involvement with the character from a preferred genre should be higher and distance should be lower compared to characters from the less preferred genres.[2] Thus, respondents who belong to the empirically grouped genre-preferences believable and unbelievable fantasy (i.e., the low-realistic genres containing the highest numbers of unrealistic features) should entail lower levels of involvement with protagonists from realistic genres. By contrast, preferences for reality registration and reality simulation should elicit higher levels of involvement with and appreciation of the protagonists from these genres than protagonists from the low-realistic genres.

Furthermore, from the popularity of "reality TV" and claims such as "story based on facts" (cf. Atkin, 1983; Berkowitz & Alioto, 1973), it may be derived that

---

[2]We envision involvement and distance as parallel processes that complement each other, not as opposing tendencies (Hoorn & Konijn, 2003; Konijn & Hoorn, in press). Therefore, we include distance as a separate variable in the analyses.

the realistic genres in general will entail a positive bias toward their protagonists. Taking the protagonist as the main carrier of the story and the genre, we hypothesize that realistic protagonists will evoke increases in the levels of involvement and appreciation compared to the unrealistic ones, even if someone prefers unbelievable fantasy. Therefore, in addition to the reality-based genre preferences, we distinguished the degree of represented reality of the character as a second experimental factor. This factor, *character-reality* (as represented), pertains to the degree to which a product portrays realistic and unrealistic features of the protagonist in a media product (thus a characteristic of the stimulus).

Method

Participants.   The participants in this study were the same 136 men and 175 women volunteers that participated in Study 1.

Stimuli.   We identified four movies as exemplars of the realistic genres (e.g., *Gandhi*) and four movies as exemplars of the unrealistic or fantasy genres (e.g., *Superman*; see Appendix). The selection of movies was based on film catalogs, encyclopedias, the CD Cinemania, Internet searches, and watching movies ourselves. The assignment to one or the other category was based on the person portrayals, the contents, and the descriptions of the feature films, in addition to the label given to them (by the producers). We focused primarily on the way in which the protagonist's features were depicted (within his or her environments) to serve the goal of our study, which guided the editing and cutting we performed (see following). To improve comparability, we restricted our choices to contemporary, original Hollywood productions in color. Each was cut back to a 20-min trailer, concentrating primarily on the main character so that each character had about equal exposure time. The trailers were captured and edited on video with the software package *Studio DC10 plus* (see details in Konijn & Hoorn, in press). The video clips did not summarize the movie as such, but rather depicted the main character in key situations.

Procedure.   Participants were asked to view a 20-min trailer of a contemporary motion picture and subsequently to answer questions about the film on a paper–pencil questionnaire (duration about 15 min). There were eight different video clips (see Appendix), in varying degrees of represented reality, which were presented to eight different groups of participants. Participants were randomly distributed over the experimental conditions of a between-subjects design. That is, each respondent only saw one of the eight clips. They watched the clips in groups of 10–20 persons, seated in a dimly lit room that mimicked a small theater. Immediately after watching the video clip, the respondents were asked to fill out the questionnaire (which was part of a larger study).

Measurements.   Measurements were developed to indicate the levels of personal involvement with, distance toward, and appreciation of the main character (10, 10, and 12 items, respectively). Each item was followed by a 6-point Likert scale ranging from 0 (*do not agree at all*) to 5 (*fully agree*). *Involvement* and *distance* were defined as the felt tendencies to (psychologically) approach and avoid the character (see Konijn & Hoorn, in press), respectively. Items reflected general positive–negative affect and approach–avoidance tendencies toward the character, such as "I want to be friends with ... ," "I feel close to ... ," "I prefer to stay away from ... ," and "... leaves me with cold feelings." The involvement scale (Cronbach's $\alpha = .90$, $M = 1.79$, $SD = .97$) also included items that could be labeled as *identification* or *empathy*. Cronbach's alpha for the distance scale was .94 ($M = 2.58$, $SD = 1.22$). *Appreciation* was operationalized in simple evaluative statements about the character, such as "... is great" and "... is boring" (Cronbach's $\alpha = .92$, $M = 2.95$, $SD = 1.03$). The three main dependent variables were interrelated. Involvement significantly correlated with appreciation, but not very strong ($r = .58$, $p < .01$, $n = 309$). Distance correlated slightly less with appreciation, but in a negative direction ($r = -.51$, $p < .01$, $n = 309$). Involvement correlated significantly and negatively with distance ($r = -.71$, $p < .01$, $n = 312$). However, one should be cautious when correlations are based on large samples because they become easily significant (Guilford, 1956).

Furthermore, to check whether the characters that we chose for their level of represented reality in the video clips were indeed perceived as such by the participants, we devised a Likert scale to measure the perceived realism of the character (Cronbach's $\alpha = .93$, $M = 2.30$, $SD = 1.08$). This factor, character-realism (as perceived), relates to the degree to which the receiver judges that reality is reflected in the protagonist of a media product. Other measurements were included, but not reported in this study (see Konijn & Hoorn, in press), as well as some control variables such as sex, age, and comprehensibility of the story.

Analyses.   To perform the statistical analyses to test the hypotheses, the respondents were grouped into four subgroups based on the variables that indicated their conventional genre preferences. These were grouped into a new variable with four values (by means of the SPSS-procedure IF), each value reflecting one of the grouped reality-based genre preferences described in Table 3. Reality-based genre preference, then, was the first independent factor to be included in a 4 × 2 multivariate analysis of variance (MANOVA). The second factor, character-reality—the degree of represented reality of the character—had two levels (realistic vs. unrealistic). The level of character-reality was based on the motion picture to which this character belonged (see Stimuli previous). Involvement, distance, and appreciation were entered as the dependent variables.

However, as can be expected, respondents marked more than one genre preference, so that certain respondents entered more than one group, whereas others did

TABLE 4
Conventional-Genre Preferences ×
Documentary Preference

Conventional-Genre Preference: Yes	Documentary Preference			
	No		Yes	
	Count	%	Count	%
Thriller	122	**69.7**	74	**54.0**
Comedy	114	65.1	84	61.3
Drama	68	**38.9**	79	**57.7**
Action	60	34.3	52	38.0
Sci-fi	41	23.4	27	19.7
Realism	71	**40.6**	81	**59.1**
Psychological	92	52.6	78	56.9
Cartoons	39	**17.7**	31	**28.5**
Romance	71	40.6	66	48.2
Horror	20	11.4	17	12.4
Other	10	5.7	14	10.2

Note. $N = 312$. Differences between preferences to conventional genres and a preference for documentaries greater than 10% are in bold. For instance, for those who prefer thriller (69.7%), 54% also prefer documentaries (considerable overlap).

not. Therefore, we used an exclusion procedure to create independent groups. For example, to be included in the reality simulation genre, a respondent should have answered *yes* to the drama, romance, or psychological genres, but also *no* to horror, thriller, cartoons, and so on (i.e., all the remaining genres).

Table 4 shows that only 3 respondents preferred documentaries alone. In other words, a genre preference for reality registration overlapped substantially with other genre preferences. To overcome the problem of not testing the documentary preferences (due to the exclusion procedure), we performed a 3 (reality-based genre preference: reality simulation vs. believable fantasy vs. unbelievable fantasy) × 2 (character-reality: realistic vs. unrealistic) MANOVA. Separately, we performed a 2 (yes vs. no preference for reality registration, i.e., documentary) × 2 (character-reality) MANOVA. All multivariate *F* values were calculated according to Pillai.

Results and Discussion

Control questions revealed that, despite editing, the plot and narrative were still comprehensible. As such, the character may be seen as the carrier of the story. The mean comprehensibility for films with realistic protagonists did not significantly differ from the mean comprehensibility of films with unrealistic protagonists in a one-way analysis (M real $= 3.63$, M unreal $= 3.75$), $F(1, 310) < 1$, scale max $= 5$. Furthermore, the selection and manipulation of the feature films reached the intended goal: Character-realism (as perceived) showed that the characters from the clips with realistic representations were indeed considered more realistic ($M = 2.43$) than the unrealistically represented characters ($M = 1.38$), and vice versa— unrealistic characters (M unreal $= 2.70$, M real $= 1.99$), $F(6, 299) = 21.19$, $p < .000$, $\eta_p^2 = .30$). Finally, sex and age only induced null effects, and sex as a covariate with reality-based genre preference by character-reality (as represented) on the three dependent variables also yielded insignificant effects ($F < 1$, $p = .79$).

The results of the 3 (reality-based genre preference: reality simulation vs. believable fantasy vs. unbelievable fantasy) $\times$ 2 (character-reality: realistic vs. unrealistic) MANOVA showed that, contrary to expectations, neither a significant main effect for reality-based genre preference, multivariate $F(6, 598) = 1.24$, $p = .29$, nor a significant interaction of reality-based genre preference with character-reality, multivariate $F(6, 598) = 1.01$, $p = .41$, was observed. However, an overall main effect was obtained for character-reality, multivariate $F(3, 298) = 6.78$, $p < .001$, $\eta_p^2 = .06$, as expected, and subsequent analyses indicated that more realistically represented characters significantly increased the levels of involvement and decreased distance toward the protagonist as compared to unrealistically represented characters. The between-subjects analyses showed, however, that the significant effects of character-reality did not hold for appreciation ($p = .148$). It appears from the means in Table 5 that the degree of represented reality of the protagonist (in its environments) induced relatively small effects (see also partial eta squared) in the predicted directions regardless of the respondent's grouped reality-based genre preferences.

Yet, the possibility still exists that, compared to other genres, documentaries have so many realistic features that they do increase the level of involvement with the pro-

TABLE 5
Mean Involvement, Distance, and Appreciation for
3 (Reality-Based Genres) $\times$ 2 (Character Reality as Represented)

| Reality-Based Genres | Involvement[a] | | | | Distance[a] | | | | Appreciation[b] | | | |
| | Realistic | | Unrealistic | | Realistic | | Unrealistic | | Realistic | | Unrealistic | |
	M	SD	M	SD	M	SD	M	SD	M	SD	M	SD
Reality simulation[b]	2.08	0.92	1.43	0.76	2.20	1.13	3.03	1.15	3.10	1.14	2.91	0.80
Believable fantasy[b]	1.88	0.87	1.70	1.00	2.56	1.21	2.77	1.16	2.98	0.98	3.00	0.97
Unbelievable fantasy[b]	2.01	1.08	1.56	1.02	2.12	1.27	2.86	1.23	2.98	1.05	2.63	1.09

Note. For realistic, $n = 43, 65, 51$ (vertically), for unrealistic, $n = 30, 71, 46$ (vertically).
[a]Indicates that differences were significant for character reality (see text). [b]Indicates no significant effects.

tagonist significantly in documentary lovers. Therefore, we contrasted the respondents who indicated preference for documentaries with those who did not. The means are presented in Table 6. A 2 (yes vs. no preference for reality registration) $\times$ 2 (character-reality) MANOVA showed overall significance for a small main effect of preference for reality registration, multivariate $F(3, 303) = 3.90, p = .009, \eta_p^2 = .04$, and for a small main effect of character-reality, multivariate $F(3, 303) = 5.25, p = .002, \eta_p^2 = .05$. However, the tests of between-subjects effects showed a significant but small main effect for preference for reality registration on distance alone, $F(1, 305) = 6.64, p = .01, \eta_p^2 = .02$. This indicates that those who like documentaries experienced a slightly lower level of distance toward the protagonists compared to those who do not prefer documentaries. No interaction effect between preference for reality registration and character-reality was found ($F < 1$). Apparently, preference for documentaries did not significantly affect personal involvement or appreciation, not even when characters were realistically depicted. Note that a decrease in distance is not the same as an increase in involvement.

In addition, we performed a separate MANOVA with the single (not grouped) conventional-genre preferences as fixed factors (11). The multivariate tests obtained no significant effects on the three dependent variables, except for the overall significance for cartoons, multivariate $F(3, 299) < 2.98, p = .032, \eta_p^2 < .030$. However, the test of between-subjects effects showed that no significant effects of cartoons was evident for the three dependent variables taken separately—that is, for involvement ($p = .473$), distance ($p = .181$), or appreciation ($p = .125$) alone.

A multiple regression analysis with the reality-based genre preferences entered in the first step as a categorical independent variable and character-reality (as represented) entered in the second step enabled further assessment of the primary genre hypothesis and clarified that the character-reality factor slightly affected the prediction of involvement and distance above and beyond genre ($R^2 = .04, \beta = -.193, p = .001; R^2 = .05, \beta = .216, p < .001$, respectively). However, no significant effects oc-

TABLE 6
Mean Involvement, Distance, and Appreciation for Preference for
2 (Reality Registration) × 2 (Character Reality as Represented)

Preference for Reality Registration[b,c]	Involvement[a]				Distance[a]				Appreciation[b]			
	Realistic		Unrealistic		Realistic		Unrealistic		Realistic		Unrealistic	
	M	SD	M	SD	M	SD	M	SD	M	SD	M	SD
Yes	2.01	1.07	1.57	0.97	2.10	1.21	2.68	1.34	3.05	1.15	2.88	1.10
No	1.92	0.84	1.62	0.95	2.55	1.19	2.94	1.06	2.95	0.94	2.90	0.95

Note. For realistic, preference yes, $n = 80$, preference no, $n = 80$. Likewise, for unrealistic, preference yes, $n = 55$, preference no, $n = 94$.
[a]Indicates that differences were significant for character reality. [b]Indicates no significant effects. [c]Indicates a significant effect on distance only (see text).

curred for appreciation ($p = .22$). Genre as a grouped variable (reality-based genre preferences) did not significantly contribute to the prediction of any of the three dependent variables. To complete the analyses, the same procedure was executed for the assessment of the effects of the separate conventional genre preferences. None of the conventional genre preferences provided a significant explanation of the variance in involvement, distance, or appreciation, except for the preference for documentaries, which provided a minor additional explanation of the variance in distance (R^2 change $= .019$, $p = .013$) in combination with character-reality. Again, the represented character-reality factor affected the prediction of involvement above and beyond the conventional genre preferences, and yet it only provided a small contribution ($R^2 = .04$, $\beta = -.186$, $p = .001$). Thus, reality representation in the character, character-reality, is the only variable in this study that significantly explained some of the variance in personal involvement of the observer with the character in a feature film. Nonetheless, this contribution is rather small.

However, the explained variance of involvement increased considerably when the perceived level of realism of a character (perceived character-realism) was entered as the second independent variable (with reality-based genre preferences as the first independent variable): for involvement, $R^2 = .20$, $\beta = .45$, $p < .001$; similarly for distance: $R^2 = .16$, $\beta = -.40$, $p < .001$. Again, the reality-based genre preferences did not show significant effects. In contrast to the represented reality in the character, the perceived level of character-realism did directly affect appreciation ($R^2 = .35$, $\beta = .59$, $p < .001$).

Contrary to expectations, then, the results of Study 2 suggest that reality-based genre preferences have no significant effect on personal involvement with, distance toward, or appreciation of protagonists from a variety of feature films. Only respondents who indicated preference for documentaries experienced somewhat less distance (but not more involvement or appreciation) toward the protagonists than respondents with other preferences. By contrast, the degree to which a character was represented as more realistic or unrealistic did evoke the expected effects, although they were small. Realistically depicted characters elicited slightly increased levels of personal involvement with the protagonist, whereas the level of distance slightly decreased, but appreciation remained unaffected. This effect was independent of genre preferences. However, the best explanation of personal involvement, distance, and appreciation, as suggested by the results of this study, was provided by the perceived level of realism of the characters above and beyond genre preference.

GENERAL DISCUSSION

In Study 1, we assessed the viability of the proposed reality-based genre taxonomy. The results showed that conventional genres could be grouped according to their representation of reality in (visual) media products. We arrived at a more parsimonious genre taxonomy of reality registration (e.g., documentary), reality sim-ulation (e.g., romance), believable fantasy (e.g., thriller), and unbelievable fantasy (e.g., sci-fi), which we then used to predict receivers' experiences of the film trail-ers. However, Study 2 showed that the reality-based genre preferences did not di-rect personal involvement with or appreciation of the protagonist. That is, when the respondent viewed a protagonist from his or her preferred genre, there was no significant increase in involvement or liking of this protagonist compared to pro-tagonists taken from the other, not-preferred genres. Only a slight decrease in the level of distance was observed for those viewers who preferred documentaries to other genres.

Instead, a realistic representation of the protagonist evoked increases in the level of involvement and decreases in distance, but did not significantly affect ap-preciation. Unrealistic characters evoked increases in the level of distance, whereas involvement decreased, and appreciation remained unaffected. More im-portant, the perceived level of character-realism made a substantial contribution to involvement, distance, and, above all, appreciation of the protagonist. Thus, en-gaging with and (dis)liking fictional characters is not so much an effect of the rep-resentation of reality in the product features, but rather of the perception of realism of those features from the perspective of the observer. This supports the arguments presented by Durkin (1985), Livingstone (1989), and Miall and Kuiken (1999) for integrating product features with the observer's response to those features.

As a form of grouping behavior and data reduction, genre taxonomies rely on the assumption that what can be attributed to the group is also valid for its members ("Sci-fi? Sure I'll like Buck Rogers"). The results presented here show that such heuristics have their limitations. We showed that a preference for a particular real-ity-based genre does not necessarily imply appreciation for the characters of that particular reality-based genre. Rather, appreciation and personal involvement are af-fected by the perceived level of realism of the character in its filmic situations, whereas the represented level of reality in the character only slightly affected in-volvement. In other words, although people may prefer sci-fi, they may still like Gandhi better than Buck Rogers if Gandhi evokes the right level of perceived reality.

Other studies have found effects of genre on experience. For instance, Heil (2002) obtained evidence for increases in state aggression, anxiety, and sadness for nonhumorous violence as compared to violent action comedy. Meade (2000) found that the motivation to watch horror was related to arousal and vicarious thrill seeking. However, these studies were either limited to one or two (sub)genres (Heil, 2002; Meade, 2000; also Buck, 1998 [silent movie]; Ordman, 1996 [trag-edy]) or concentrated on some negative emotions (aggression, anxiety, sadness in Heil, 2002; anger and crying in Ordman, 1996; arousal and thrill seeking in Meade, 2000). In our Study 2, we also found that only one genre, documentary, slightly affected negative experiences (distance), although in a positive direction (a decrease in distance). Together, the evidence seems to converge and perhaps sug-gests that "negative" genres, such as horror and violent action, have effects on "negative" experiences, whereas the positive aspects (e.g., humor) only mitigate negativity. This is in line with Buck's report that the effects of a silent film classic on psychological involvement and aesthetic preference were insignificant. With Cohen and Weimann (2000), then, we emphasize that "some genres have some effects on some viewers," primarily in the "negative" genre segment and with respect to "negative" emotions.

Reality TV, VR, and docusoaps capitalize on the assumption that adding more reality to their products will boost involvement and appreciation in the receiver. Our sense of "being-there" (cf. presence), however, can be induced by reading a book just as easily as by using new technology. We think this is the case because the perceived (psychological) realism of the character's actions, feelings, thoughts, and so on, is more important than the "reality" of the technical representation of the character. For instance, a VR environment that displays a character who is not "real" is not something with which a user can emotionally connect (cf. Bailenson, Blascovich, Beall, & Loomis, 2003; Blascovich et al., 2002; Monk & Gale, 2002). However, a book character that acts in a way readers can grasp will be observed, judged, liked, or resented. Likewise, our studies suggest that increasing the number and quality of realistic representations (as product features) may not increase preference for such genres, nor do they enhance the degree of involvement with and appreciation of the characters that much (cf. Hoorn et al., 2003). In contrast, the perception of the level of realism partly determines involvement and appreciation and points at the active role of the viewer. To trigger the desired experience in their audiences, then, creators of reality-based genres should have a firm understanding of how different audiences experience mediated reality. In this sense, the Aristotelian proposal that an increase in the number of realistic features engenders increased involvement in the receiver may only hold if those features are perceived as realistic. An interesting question for future studies is how strictly genre or style conventions set the parameters for the "right" degree of realism in the eyes of the observer.

Although genre preferences apparently do not increase involvement with the protagonist (e.g., experiencing friendship, sympathy, and intimacy), it might well be that they evoke personal emotions that are not captured by involvement with the character. Happiness, sadness, and suspense, for example, can be evoked by personal reminiscences, certain cinematic and narrative techniques, or the plot (e.g., Vorderer, 2000). Thus, certain genres may boost certain emotions, but experiencing emotions does not necessarily mean that they involve the viewer with the character. Perhaps genre may affect appreciation for narrative structure and plot (although Buck, 1998, found no evidence), but engagement with and appreciation of the character in its situations may be independent from that. Although the perceived realism of the protagonist apparently is predictive of involvement, the question remains whether the protagonist is a determinant of genre attribution, as Zubarev (1999) suggested. In our results, we find a suggestion that the main character has a central position for understanding the plot, because the respondents reported that they could easily follow the story despite the serious editing that we did. However, although the character may be seen as the carrier of the story, a question for future research is to what degree characters are fundamental to establishing genres.

Hence, the question remains whether it is fruitful to produce a taxonomy based on a receiver's perspective. On the one hand, the reality-based genre taxonomy designed for the study presented here is supported by empirical data—that is, by grouping individual genre preferences. Thus, it seems to make sense to group cultural products in a more parsimonious way on a criterion that is relevant to the receivers. Somehow, viewers' implicit grouping behavior for feature films seems to be reflected in statistically grouping their preferences for single, conventional genres. Furthermore, confronting the theoretically devised reality-based genre taxonomy based on product features with the empirical data from a receiver's perspective prompted a regrouping of some aspects of the taxonomy. The results are in line with a recent study of Nabi, Biely, Morgan, and Stitt (2003), who found a reality–fiction dimension as the only stable dimension in respondents' grouping of television programs.

On the other hand, it does not seem useful to establish a reality-based genre taxonomy because it has no effects on a principal element of viewers' personal involvement with and appreciation of the protagonists. In this respect, therefore, it seems as if designing a taxonomy from a reader's/viewer's perspective is not very useful in predicting the viewer's responses. However, the degree of (un)realistic representation of the protagonist (including its situational features) will have a small but significant effect on personal involvement, such that a more realistic character increases involvement, but not appreciation. Yet, the explanatory power of the represented reality criterion at the product side appeared to be limited, so that we have to look for other factors as well. Studies in affective disposition theory have repeatedly shown that the moral judgment of a character, whether he or she is a good hero or a bad villain, is important to engaging with characters (e.g., Raney & Bryant, 2002; Zillmann, 1994; Zillmann & Cantor, 1977) both in fiction and nonfiction (Zillmann, Taylor, & Lewis, 1998; see also Bryant, Roskos-Ewoldsen, & Cantor, 2003). Furthermore, studies in art perception (e.g., Cupchik, 1997; Dion, Berscheid, & Walster, 1972) and interpersonal attraction (e.g., Baker & Churchill, 1977; Iannucci, 1992) emphasize that aesthetic appeal is an important contributing factor to (art) appreciation. In her correlational studies, Buck (1998) found that, among others, the subscales of aesthetic preference and psychological involvement were strongly correlated and that they contributed to one another. The effects of the triad morality (ethics), beauty (aesthetics), and realism (epistemics) on personal involvement with fictional characters are examined in Konijn and Hoorn (in press).

All in all, the results of our studies show that it is worthwhile to take the active role of the reader/viewer into consideration in studying media effects and to arrive at integrative theories and empirical validation of interaction processes between product features and receiver's interpretations of a cultural product. Our results are in line with what Miall and Kuiken (1999) proposed in their search for "literariness"—the interaction between objective features of the text and the reader's response to those features. Creating genre taxonomies or new genre labels based on product or content features may have its usefulness from a producer's perspective. However, from a receiver's perspective, other, more experiential or psychological dimensions seem to contribute to their personal involvement and liking of specific characters appearing in such genres. Clearly, readers/viewers do not simply take over the genre convention per se, but they make up their own minds. For instance, absurd action in *Monty Python's Life of Brian* (Jones, 1979) may provoke involvement with the protagonist not because the level of represented reality is low, but rather because the level of its perceived realism is high. In this respect, character attributes might well fulfill key roles in determining the perceived realism of a program, movie, or text, even when they appear in completely fictitious settings. It may be interesting in future research to study how perceived realism of a character in various fictitious settings may determine the perceived realism of the media presentation as a whole and how involvement with a protagonist relates to discrete emotional responses.

ACKNOWLEDGMENTS

This study is partly done within the ASPASIA-project of Elly A. Konijn, facilitated by the Faculty of Social Sciences, Dept. of Communication Science, at the Free University of Amsterdam (NWO File No. 015.000.019). It is also supported by a grant to Elly A. Konijn and Johan F. Hoorn from the Netherlands Organization of Scientific Research (NWO File No. 301–80–79b).

REFERENCES

Atkin, C. (1983). Effects of realistic TV violence vs. fictional violence on aggression. *Journalism Quarterly, 60,* 615–621.

Bailenson, J. N., Blascovich, J., Beall, A. C., & Loomis, J. M. (2003). Interpersonal distance in immersive virtual environments. *Personality and Social Psychology Bulletin, 29,* 819–833.

Baker, M. J., & Churchill, G. A. (1977). The impact of physically attractive models on advertising evaluations. *Journal of Marketing Research, 14,* 538–555.

Bazin, A. (1962). *Qu'est-ce que le cinéma? IV. Une esthétique de la réalité* [What is cinema? IV. Aesthetics of reality]. Paris: Cerf.

Berkowitz, L., & Alioto, J. T. (1973). The meaning of an observed event as a determinant of its aggressive consequences. *Journal of Personality and Social Psychology, 28,* 206–217.

Blascovich, J., Loomis, J., Beall, A. C., Swinth, K. R., Hoyt, C. L., & Bailenson, J. N. (2002). Immersive virtual environment technology as a methodological tool for social psychology. *Psychological Inquiry, 13,* 103–124.

Book Nuts Reading Club. (2003). Retrieved August 22, 2003, from http://www.booknutsreadingclub.com/genrelist.html

Bordwell, D. (1989). *Making meaning: Inference and rhetoric in the interpretation of cinema.* Cambridge, MA: Harvard University Press.

Bordwell, D., Staiger, J., & Thompson, K. (1985). *The classical Hollywood cinema: Film style and mode of production.* New York: Columbia University Press.

Bryant, J., Roskos-Ewoldsen, D., & Cantor, J. (Eds.). (2003). *Communication and emotion: Essays in honor of Dolf Zillmann.* Mahwah, NJ: Lawrence Erlbaum Associates, Inc.

Buck, J. R. (1998). Psychological meaning: The effects of genre and context on narrative structure (Doctoral dissertation, Long Island University, 1998). *Dissertation Abstracts International, 59,* 0433.

Chandler, D. (2000). *An introduction to genre theory.* Retrieved January 29, 2003, from http://www.aber.ac.uk/media/Documents/intgenre/intgenre1.html

Cohen, J., & Weimann, G. (2000). Cultivation revisited: Some genres have some effects on some viewers. *Communication Reports, 13,* 99–114.

Cupchik, G. C. (1997). Identification as a basic problem for aesthetic reception. In S. Tötösy de Zepetnek & I. Sywenky (Eds.), *The systemic and empirical approach to literature and culture as theory and application* (pp. 11–22). Edmonton, Canada: University of Alberta, Edmonton.

Davies, M. M. (1997). *Fake, fact, and fantasy: Children's interpretation of television reality.* Mahwah, NJ: Lawrence Erlbaum Associates, Inc.

Dillman, D. A. (1979). *Mail and telephone surveys; the total design method.* New York: Wiley-Interscience.

Dion, K. K., Berscheid, E., & Walster, E. (1972). What is beautiful is good. *Journal of Personality and Social Psychology, 24,* 285–290.

Dirks, T. (2002). *Film genres.* Retrieved January 29, 2003, from http://www.filmsite.org/genres.html

Durkin, K. (1985). Television and sex-role acquisition 1: Content. *British Journal of Social Psychology, 24,* 101–113.

Fitch, M., Huston, A. C., & Wright, J. C. (1993). From television forms to genre schemata: Children's perceptions of television reality. In G. L. Berry & J. K. Asamen (Eds.), *Children and television: Images in a changing sociocultural world* (pp. 38–52). Thousand Oaks, CA: Sage.

Freedman, A., & Medway, P. (1994). Locating genre studies: Antecedents and prospects. In A. Freedman & P. Medway (Eds.), *Genre and the new rhetoric* (pp. 1–20). London: Taylor & Francis.

Gerbner, G., Gross, L., Morgan, M., & Signorielli, N. (1994). Growing up with television: The cultivation perspective. In J. Bryant & D. Zillmann (Eds.), *Media effects: Advances in theory and research* (pp. 17–40). Hillsdale, NJ: Lawrence Erlbaum Associates, Inc.

Grodal, T. K. (2000). Subjectivity, objectivity and aesthetic feelings in film. In I. Bondebjerg (Ed.), *Moving images, culture and the mind* (pp. 87–104). Luton, England: University of Luton Press.

Guilford, J. P. (1956). *Fundamental statistics in psychology and education.* New York: McGraw-Hill.

Gunter, B., & Furham, A. (1984). Perceptions of television violence: Effects of programme genre and type of violence on viewers' judgements of violent portrayals. *British Journal of Social Psychology, 23,* 155–164.

Heil, S. K. R. (2002). Does humor mediate the effects of film violence? Affective consequences of viewing violent action comedy (Doctoral dissertation, Kansas State University, 2002). *Dissertation Abstracts International, 62,* 3420. (UMI No. AAI3019359)

Hoffner, C., & Cantor, J. (1991). Perceiving and responding to media characters. In J. Bryant & D. Zillmann (Eds.), *Responding to the screen: Reception and reaction processes* (chap. 4, pp. 63–101). Hillsdale, NJ: Lawrence Erlbaum Associates, Inc.

Hoorn, J. F., & Konijn, E. A. (2003). Perceiving and experiencing fictional characters: An integrative account. *Japanese Psychological Research, 45,* 221–239.

Hoorn, J. F., Konijn, E. A., & Van der Veer, G. C. (2003, February 15). Virtual reality: Do not augment realism, augment relevance. *Upgrade (Human-Computer Interaction: Overcoming Barriers), 4,* 18–26. Retrieved February 15, 2003, from http://www.upgrade-cepis.org/issues/2003/1/up4–1Hoorn.pdf

Horton, D., & Wohl, R. R. (1986). Mass communication and para-social interaction. Observation on intimacy at a distance. In G. Gumpert & R. Cathcart (Eds.), *Inter media: Interpersonal communication in a media world* (3rd ed., pp. 185–206). New York: Oxford University Press. (Original work published 1956)

Iannucci, A. (1992). Patterns of consensus and divergence in the judgment of personality traits among a group of well-acquainted young women. *Dissertation Abstracts International, 52,* 4384–4385.

Jaccard, P. (1908). Nouvelles recherches sur la distribution florale [New investigations into floral distribution]. *Bulletin Société Vaudoise des Sciences Naturelles, 44,* 223–270.

Jones, T. (Director). (1979). *Monty Python's Life of Brian* [Motion Picture]. England.

Konijn, E. A. (1999). Spotlight on spectators: Emotions in the theater. *Discourse Processes, 28,* 169–194.

Konijn, E. A. (2000). *Acting emotions.* Amsterdam: Amsterdam University Press.

Konijn, E. A., & Hoorn, J. F. (in press). Some like it bad. Testing a model for perceiving and experiencing fictional characters. *Media Psychology.*

Kracauer, S. (1960). *Theory of film. The redemption of physical reality.* New York: Oxford University Press.

Livingstone, S. M. (1989). Interpretive viewers and structured programs. *Communication Research, 16,* 25–57.

Livingstone, S. M. (1990). *Making sense of television: The psychology of audience interpretation.* London: Pergamon.

Mallon, T. (2002). History, fiction, and the burden of truth. *Writing history/writing fiction: A virtual conference session.* History and MultiMedia Center, University at Albany. Retrieved August 19, 2003, from http://www.albany.edu/history/hist_fict/Mallon/Mallons.htm

Martindale, C. (1996). A note on the relationship between prototypicality and preference. *Empirical Studies of the Arts, 14,* 109–113.

McGhee, P. E., & Goldstein, J. H. (Eds.). (1983). *Handbook of humor research: Vol. 1. Basic Issues.* New York: Springer.

Meade, B. (2000). Adult motivations for viewing horror films (Doctoral dissertation, University of Kansas, 2000). *Dissertation Abstracts International, 60,* 2717.

Miall, D. S., & Kuiken, D. (1998). The form of reading: Empirical studies of literariness. *Poetics, 25,* 327–341.

Miall, D. S., & Kuiken, D. (1999). What is literariness? Three components of literary reading. *Discourse Processes, 28,* 121–138.

Milligan, G. W., & Schilling, D. A. (1985). Asymptotic and finite sample characteristics of four external criterion measures. *Multivariate Behavioral Research, 20,* 97–109.

Monk, A. F., & Gale, C. (2002). A look is worth a thousand words: Full gaze awareness in video-mediated conversation. *Discourse Processes, 33,* 257–278.

Nabi, R. L., Biely, E. N., Morgan, S. J., & Stitt, C. R. (2003). Reality-based television programming and the psychology of its appeal. *Media Psychology, 5,* 303–330.

Nichols, B. (1991). *Blurred boundaries: Questions of meaning in contemporary culture.* Bloomington: Indiana University Press.

Nowlan, P. F. (1928, August). Armageddon-2419 A.D. *Amazing Stories.*

Oatley, K. (1994). A taxonomy of the emotions of literary response and a theory of identification in fictional narrative. *Poetics, 23,* 53–74.

Oatley, K. (1999). Why fiction may be twice as true as fact: Fiction as cognitive and emotional simulation. *Review of General Psychology, 3,* 101–117.

Oosterveld, P. (1996). *Questionnaire design methods.* Nijmegen, The Netherlands: Berkhout.

Ordman, V. V. (1996). Effects of exposure to tragedy as filmed entertainment of anger in men and women: Is crying cathartic? (Doctoral dissertation, University of Alabama, 1996). *Dissertation Abstracts International, 57,* 2255.

Piters, R. A. M. P., & Stokmans, M. J. W. (2000). Genre categorization and its effect on preference for fiction books. *Empirical Studies of the Arts, 18,* 159–166.

Raney, A. A., & Bryant, J. (2002). Moral judgment and crime drama: An integrated theory of enjoyment. *Journal of Communication, 52*(2), 402–415.

Ruch, W. (1993). Exhilaration and humor. In M. Lewis & J. N. Haviland (Eds.), *Handbook of emotion* (pp. 605–616). New York: Guilford.

Schatz, T. (1981). *Hollywood genres: Formulas, filmmaking and the studio system.* Philadelphia: Temple University Press.

Shapiro, M. A., & McDonald, D. G. (1992). I'm not a real doctor, but I play one in virtual reality: Implications of virtual reality for judgments about reality. *Journal of Communication, 42*(4), 95–114.

Smith, M. (1995). *Engaging characters. Fiction, emotion, and the cinema.* Oxford, England: Clarendon.

Steen, G. J. (1999). Genres of discourse and the definition of literature. *Discourse Processes, 28,* 109–120.

Tan, E. S.-H. (1996). *Emotion and the structure of narrative film. Film as an emotion machine.* Mahwah, NJ: Lawrence Erlbaum Associates, Inc.

Vorderer, P. (2000). Entertainment, suspense, and interactivity. In I. Bondebjerg (Ed.), *Moving images, culture and the mind* (pp. 65–83). Luton, England: University of Luton Press.

Zillmann, D. (1994). Mechanisms of emotional involvement with drama. *Poetics, 23,* 33–51.

Zillmann, D. (1996). The psychology of suspense in dramatic exposition. In P. Vorderer, H. J. Wulff, & M. Friedrichsen (Eds.), *Suspense: Conceptualizations, theoretical analyses, and empirical explorations* (pp. 199–231). Mahwah, NJ: Lawrence Erlbaum Associates, Inc.

Zillmann, D. (2002). Exemplification theory of media influence. In J. Bryant & D. Zillmann (Eds.), *Media effects: Advances in theory and research* (2nd ed., pp. 19–42). Hillsdale, NJ: Lawrence Erlbaum Associates, Inc.

Zillmann, D., & Cantor, J. R. (1977). Affective response to the emotions of a protagonist. *Journal of Experimental Social Psychology, 13,* 155–165.

Zillmann, D., Taylor, K., & Lewis, K. (1998). News as nonfiction theater: How dispositions toward the public cast of characters affect reactions. *Journal of Broadcasting and Electronic Media, 42,* 153–169.

Zubarev, V. (1999). The comic in literature as a general systems phenomenon. *CLCWeb: Comparative Literature and Culture: A WWWeb Journal 1.1.* Retrieved December 21, 2002, from http://www.arts.ualberta.ca/clcwebjournal/clcweb99–1/zubarev99.html

APPENDIX

Fictional Character	Performer	Film	Year	Director	Represented Reality of the Character	Min	n
Mahatma Gandhi	Ben Kingsley	*Gandhi*	1982	Richard Attenborough	Realistic	20:36	39
Bridget Gregory	Linda Fiorentino	*The Last Seduction*	1994	John Dahl	Realistic	22:02	40
Rocky Dennis	Eric Stoltz	*Mask*	1985	Peter Bogdanovich	Realistic	21:15	42
John Sedley	Mickey Rourke	*Johnny Handsome*	1989	Walter Hill	Realistic	18:38	39
Superman	Christopher Reeve	*Superman*	1978	Richard Donner	Unrealistic	22:53	36
Cruella de Vil	Glenn Close	*101 Dalmatians*	1996	Stephen Herek	Unrealistic	21:10	37
Edward Scissorhands	Johnny Depp	*Edward Scissorhands*	1990	Tim Burton	Unrealistic	21:47	38
Count Vlad Dracul	Gary Oldman	*Bram Stoker's Dracula*	1992	Francis Ford Coppola	Unrealistic	18:12	41

Note. Mohandas K. Gandhi: At first a lawyer in South Africa, then becomes India's leader of nonviolent resistance against British oppression. Nowadays, a worldwide symbol of peace and understanding. Bridget Gregory: Extremely attractive woman deceives her husband, runs off with the money from a drug deal they set up, lands at a small town where she seduces a boyish lover to kill her revenge-seeking husband, faking a rape to turn the boy in to the police. Rocky Dennis: Adolescent boy suffers from craniodiaphyseal dysplasia, a disease that causes the disfigurement of his face. He succeeds at doing the right thing in a world of Hell's Angels, drug abuse, and misdemeanors. Finds love in the arms of a blind girl who sees his inner beauty. John Sedley: Small-time criminal with a skull forced out of shape (nickname Johnny Handsome) is imprisoned after his fellow lowlifes have deserted him. A plastic surgeon proposes to help him prove the theory that normal looks will normalize behavior. The doctor is proven wrong. Superman: Supernatural mister righteous stays modest and polite while flying around arresting criminals, fixing cracks in the earth, and avoiding the flooding of a town. His love for Lois Lane brings him to breaking his vow not to interfere with earth's history but this is all for the best. He says he is for "truth, justice, and the American Way." Cruella de Vil:. Runs a fashion house with extravagance and wickedness. Her latest craze is to have a coat of dalmatian puppy fur. All dalmatian doggies of London are kidnapped but the spectacular fashion witch bites the dust after all, due to the willful scheming of animated animals. Edward Scissorhands: Feeble and unadapted to normal life, the Frankenstein-like boy with scissors for hands is adopted by a kindhearted Avon Lady, who wants him to look beautiful again. American suburbia thinks differently and scams him into a burglery but he survives social abandonment and keeps straight. Count Vlad Dracul: Old Romanian warlord rises from the dead to defy Christ and avenge the death of his wife. Finds her mirror image in Victorian London, a lovely young woman who cannot resist his seductive shrewdness. The gruesome vampire wants her living blood to take her with him into eternal doom.

DISCOURSE PROCESSES, *38*(2), 247–266

Transportation Into Narrative Worlds: The Role of Prior Knowledge and Perceived Realism

Melanie C. Green

Department of Psychology, University of Pennsylvania

"Transportation into a narrative world" (Green & Brock, 2000, 2002) has been identified as a mechanism of narrative impact. A transported individual is cognitively and emotionally involved in the story and may experience vivid mental images. In the study reported here, undergraduate participants ($N = 152$) read a narrative about a homosexual man attending his college fraternity reunion, rated their transportation into the story, rated the perceived realism of the story, and responded to statements describing story-relevant beliefs. Transportation was positively correlated with perceived realism. Furthermore, individuals with prior knowledge or experience relevant to the themes of the story (e.g., had homosexual friends or family members, were knowledgeable about American fraternities) showed greater transportation into the story. Highly transported readers showed more story-consistent beliefs, and the positive relationship between transportation and story-consistent beliefs held for those both with and without previous relevant experience.

Narratives have the power to sweep readers away to different places and times or to alternative universes. Readers of compelling stories may lose track of time, fail to observe events going on around them, and feel that they are completely immersed in the world of the narrative. We call this process "transportation into a narrative world" and suggest that transportation may be a key mechanism of narrative impact (Green & Brock, 2000, 2002). Individuals' immersion in a work of literature may allow the implications of the narrative to become part of the reader's real-life beliefs.

Because transportation can lead to belief change, it is important to explore factors that influence when individuals will become transported into a narrative, as

---

Correspondence and requests for reprints should be sent to Melanie C. Green, University of Pennsylvania, Department of Psychology, 3720 Walnut Street, Philadelphia, PA 19104. E-mail: mcgreen@psych.upenn.edu.

well as the means by which transportation leads to real-world belief change. The study reported here focused on two questions. The first was whether prior familiarity with issues or themes in the story would increase individuals' tendency to become transported into the narrative. The second was whether transportation would increase perceptions of realism, and if so, whether these perceptions mediate the effect of transportation on beliefs. To test the mediation hypothesis, we attempted to manipulate transportation directly, through prereading instructions.

TRANSPORTATION INTO NARRATIVE WORLDS

Transportation is defined as an integrative melding of attention, imagery, and feelings, focused on story events (Green & Brock, 2000; see also Gerrig, 1993; Nell, 1988). Transportation, psychologically similar to flow (Csikszentmihalyi, 1990) or absorption (Tellegen, 1982), is a form of experiential response to narratives (Prentice & Gerrig, 1999). A transported reader suspends normal assumptions and treats the narrative as the frame of reference (see Strange, 2002).

Like a literal traveler, the transported reader loses access to aspects of the world of origin (see Gerrig, 1993). In other words, the reader may consciously or unconsciously push real-world facts aside and instead engage the narrative world created by the author. Previous research has shown that individuals who are transported into a narrative world are likely to change their real-world beliefs and attitudes in response to information, claims, or events in a story. For example, transported readers of a story about an attack on a small girl at a shopping mall were more likely than their less transported counterparts to believe that malls were dangerous places and that the world was unjust (Green & Brock, 2000). Transportation was also associated with increased positivity toward sympathetic characters and a reduction in negative thoughts about story content. These findings have been replicated with both measured and manipulated differences in transportation.

The phenomenological experience of being lost in a book may produce belief change in several ways: reducing negative cognitive responding, creating attachments to or feelings for characters, and making the narrative world seem more real and narrative events more like personal experience. The study reported here focuses on the latter mechanism of belief change: increased realism. (Figure 1 summarizes our model of these processes.)

TRANSPORTATION AND LITERARINESS

For transportation to occur, some narrative world must be created; characters and settings must be evoked, not merely emotions (see Green & Brock, 2002). Previ-

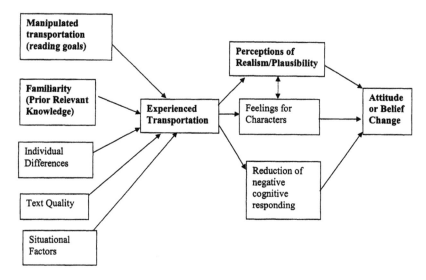

FIGURE 1   Antecedents and consequences of transportation into a narrative world (elements tested in the study reported here indicated in bold).

ous research suggests that writing quality influences transportation; bestsellers and classic short stories are rated as more transporting than narratives created by psychologists for experimental purposes (Green & Brock, 2000). However, a piece of fiction does not necessarily have to have strongly literary features to be transporting; a formulaic thriller, for example, also can effectively draw individuals into its world. However, literature may be more likely to lead to transformations of the self (Miall & Kuiken, 2002; Oatley, 2002), in addition to changes in story-related beliefs (cf. Ottati, Rhoads, & Graesser, 1999), particularly when individuals are transported (see Kuiken et al., this issue). Although the story used in the study reported here has some literary elements (as described following), these elements per se are not the focus of the investigation presented here.

BECOMING TRANSPORTED:
MANIPULATED TRANSPORTATION

Transportation has proven somewhat resistant to manipulations that do not involve changes in the text itself; however, previous research has shown that prereading instructions that induce a focus on surface aspects of a text can successfully lower transportation relative to baseline (Green & Brock, 2000). The study reported here describes a new attempt to increase transportation through relaxation instructions to participants. We expected that these instructions would create an openness that might facilitate transportation. The study also presents a new attempt to reduce transportation. Specifically, we tried to create a low-transportation condition by inducing a critical or elaborative mindset. We expected that individuals who are evaluating the claims of a story will be less likely to become transported because their cognitive resources are committed to their critique of the author. Hypothesis 1, then, is that prereading instructions can increase or decrease transportation into a narrative relative to a no-instruction control group. A successful manipulation of transportation would allow a more direct test of the mediating role of perceived realism on the endorsement of story-relevant beliefs, as described following.

BECOMING TRANSPORTED: ROLE OF PREVIOUS KNOWLEDGE

In addition to manipulating transportation, we wanted to investigate the role of individual differences in reader background that might influence transportation—specifically, background that might affect the reader's ability to relate to a character's situation. We hypothesized that knowing a real-life person who shared a significant characteristic with the main character (in the study reported here, sexual orientation) would increase the likelihood that individuals would be transported. Similarly, Zillmann (1991, 1994) proposed that, in response to drama, individuals whose moral judgments are congruent with a character's become more involved in the narrative (e.g., by becoming more empathically and affectively engaged). Although Zillmann's disposition theory focuses on moral judgments, we propose that other pre-existing sources of similarity may enhance involvement as well.[1]

We also predicted that prior knowledge about one of the main topics of the story (here, the fraternity system in the United States) would increase reader transportation. Individuals who have prior familiarity with story themes may be more motivated to immerse themselves in the story due to intrinsic interest or may have an easier time imagining story events. Larsen and Laszlo (1990) presented evidence that cultural proximity to the story world (i.e., possessing cultural–historical knowledge relevant to story themes) led to more positive story evaluations. Individuals who had this pre-existing knowledge also reported more remindings of vivid and personally experienced events in response to the story. Similarly, Braun and Cupchik (2001) suggested that differences in familiarity evoke different reading processes. Individuals can understand familiar experiences that occur in texts by creating a parallel experience. These readers may be able to draw on prior expe-

---

[1]It is possible that moral judgments may have indirectly played a role in the study reported here. Specifically, individuals who did not have a close friend or family member who was homosexual may have been more likely to believe that homosexuality is sinful and morally wrong.

rience to understand the feelings of the characters, and this may deepen their transportation into the text. On the other hand, Braun and Cupchik proposed that readers encountering a relatively unfamiliar situation focus on description and symbolic meaning. These readers may be more distanced from the reading experience because of the work needed to create an understanding of the events.

Vorderer, Knobloch, and Schramm (2001) manipulated a type of familiarity in their study of interactive media. Half of their sample saw an introduction that gave background information about the protagonist, whereas the other half saw information that did not create such a parasocial relationship. They found that their manipulation increased sympathy for the main character at an initial measurement, but that this increase did not last through the entire media exposure. The study reported here extends these findings by examining familiarity based on previous experience. This type of familiarity is likely to be more powerful, because the individuals can draw on their own rich store of personal experience rather than relying solely on recently obtained information.

Hypothesis 2, then, is that familiarity with story-relevant information (in the study reported here, either having a gay friend or family member or being knowledgeable about the fraternity system) will increase transportation.

TRANSPORTATION, REALISM, AND BELIEFS

We also explored the relationships between transportation, perceived realism, and belief change. As noted previously, one means by which transportation may affect beliefs is by making narrative events seem more like personal experience. Research has shown that direct experience with attitude objects can result in strong and enduring attitudes (see Fazio & Zanna, 1981, for a review). Similarly, if a reader feels that she has experienced realistic narrative events, the lessons implied by those events may seem more powerful. The reader may know that the story events did not actually happen, but may nonetheless experience real emotions and believe that similar events could actually happen. Research on source monitoring suggests that imagined events may be misremembered as real to the extent that the memories have qualities similar to real memories—for example, concreteness and vivid detail (Johnson, Hastroudi, & Lindsay, 1993). Narratives, particularly ones into which readers have become transported, are likely to meet those criteria.

Realism Versus Fact

Perceived realism is not to be confused with the real-world truth value of a story. Studies suggest that the real-world truth value of a story has little impact on the extent to which readers become engaged in it, enjoy it, and are affected by it. Individuals may become equally transported into factual and fictional narratives, and indeed, fictional narratives can change beliefs as much as factual ones (Green & Brock, 2000; see also Prentice, Gerrig, & Bailis, 1997; Slater, 1990; Strange & Leung, 1999; Wheeler, Green, & Brock, 1999). The reason may be that, as Bruner (1986) claimed, stories are treated differently from scientific or logical argument and may be held to different truth standards than rhetorical messages. More recently, Oatley (1999) expressed a similar view, concluding that fiction "may be twice as true as fact" (p. 101).

Here, we were not interested in the actual truth status of the story (fiction vs. nonfiction); rather, we were interested in individuals' subjective evaluations of the plausibility and realism of story events, settings, and characters. We hypothesized that the story would seem more plausible to individuals who are transported into it—that is, that the narrative world would seem more like the actual world to a transported reader (Hypothesis 3).[2]

Furthermore, previous research, particularly focusing on television, indicates that perceived realism can affect belief change (e.g., Busselle & Greenberg, 2000; Potter, 1988). So, consistent with prior studies (Green & Brock, 2000), we predicted that transported readers would show greater endorsement of story-consistent beliefs (Hypothesis 4). Even more specifically, we hypothesized that perceptions of realism should mediate the relationship between transportation and belief change; that is, in a structural model, the magnitude of the direct path between transportation and beliefs should be reduced when realism is entered into the equation (Hypothesis 5; Baron & Kenny, 1986).

Style and Realism

Stylistic aspects of a narrative may increase or decrease perceptions of realism. For example, Shapiro and Chock (2003) presented evidence that the inclusion of more typical information in a media presentation led to increases in perceived realism. In the study reported here, the narrative was written in a relatively realistic style; there was nothing fantastical or supernatural about any of the story events. However, transported readers may be especially responsive to those stylistic variations that are the source of realism. As Oatley (1999) noted, literature typically does not attempt to create an exact copy of actual occurrences or conversations. Rather, literature gains its truth by creating a simulation of the essential aspects of human life. Literature provides meaning and context, presenting events in a coherent structure. In this view, some stories seem realistic because they provide this coherence. And, transportation may increase perceptions of coherence because individ-

---

[2]Of course, the reverse relation is also possible; it could be easier to become transported into a narrative that seems plausible. The relationship may also be bidirectional, such that a story may have to meet some minimum level of psychological plausibility for readers to become transported into it, but once individuals are transported, the story may come to seem even more realistic.

uals may be more likely to create rich mental pictures of characters, anticipate story events, and provide imaginative investment to flesh out the narrative world.

Emotions and Realism

A second kind of truth in fiction, according to Oatley (1999), is personal truth or insight. This insight is most likely to occur when emotions are evoked by the narrative (and when the narrative helps the reader to understand those emotions.) Transportation also may lead to an increase in this second kind of truth, because a transported reader is more likely to experience strong emotions in response to the text. Consistent with this proposal, Hoorn, Konijn, and Van der Veer (2003) argued that *emotional relevance*, or involvement with the content of a story, is more important than literal realism in encouraging immersion. In a virtual reality paradigm, for example, it may be more important to have psychologically compelling characters than that those characters look like actual human beings (rather than cartoons). Transportation theory proposes that feelings for characters may be an independent mechanism for belief changes, but these emotional responses may also contribute to perceived realism. The realism measure used in this study taps a type of plausibility that is closer to this emotional relevance—for example, by asking about whether the characters acted like real people would act.

OVERVIEW

The study reported here was thus designed to address (a) the effect of prereading instructions on transportation into a story, (b) the role of prior knowledge and experience in individuals' tendencies to become transported into a narrative, (c) the effect of transportation on perceived realism, (d) the effect of transportation on story-related beliefs, and (e) the mediating role of perceived realism in the endorsement of story-consistent beliefs.

To examine these issues, undergraduate participants read a (slightly adapted) short story, "Just as I Am," by best-selling author E. L. Harris (1996). The story is told in first-person perspective from the point of view of a homosexual man who returns to his college fraternity reunion, where none of his former fraternity brothers know that he is gay. Before reading, participants were given instructions about how to approach the reading task. After reading, participants rated their transportation into the story, reported how realistic the story seemed to them, and responded to belief statements implied by the story. They also provided information about their own experiences relevant to the story, including friendships with homosexuals and knowledge about the fraternity system.

METHOD

Participants

Undergraduates ($N = 152$; 65 men and 87 women) participated in small groups in exchange for psychology course credit. Participants ranged from 18 to 21 years of age ($M = 18.83$, $SD = .96$).

Materials

Experimental narrative: "Just as I Am" (Harris, 1996).   The narrative (approximately 3,800 words long) is a first-person account of a gay man returning to his college fraternity for a reunion and encountering homophobia among current fraternity members. The story highlights the difficulties faced by gay men, particularly in fraternity settings, and ends with the attempted suicide of a potential fraternity member who had been harassed by current members because of his sexual orientation. The story also addresses issues related to pledging (joining) a fraternity and hazing, as well as the relationships between alumni and current fraternity members. The story was chosen because it contains compelling prose, addresses topics of interest to students, and has implications for measurable beliefs.

Much of "Just as I Am" (Harris, 1996) involves the thoughts and feelings of the main character. A typical passage reads: "My stomach churned. I was thinking about this young gay whom I didn't know and what would have happened to me if people had discovered my doubts about my sexuality before pledging" (p. 494). Although much of the writing is straightforward, plain language, there are also some elements of foregrounding—stylistic effects that allow the author to evoke feeling and make the familiar strange (e.g., Miall & Kuiken, 1994). For example, the story begins with a description of the seasons:

> I love fall weather. Cool, crisp nights watching the summer try to hold on until fall's colorful foliage forces its hand and sends it packing. But there was something different about the beginning of this fall that led me to believe this year's would not be the same. They say winter is the season of discontent, but sometimes discontent comes early. (p. 487)

The story, then, has literary elements, but is not stylistically complicated.

Instruction set (transportation) manipulation.   Participants were randomly assigned to transportation, elaboration, or control instruction conditions. These prereading instructions encouraged participants to either become more transported ("As we are interested in your natural responses to the passage, please try to relax and read the narrative as if you were leisurely reading a story in the comfort of your home") or consider critically the story content ("think carefully about the arguments, statements and beliefs the characters and settings seem to depict"). Transportation and elaboration participants were given a brief reminder about their instructions on a page inserted after the first two pages of the story. Control condition participants received no specific instructions about how to approach the reading task. Participants completed the following dependent measures in the order described following.

Belief statements.   Participants responded to a series of belief statements related to themes or assertions in the story. All statements were rated on a 1 (*strongly disagree*) to 7 (*strongly agree*) scale. From these items, we created four belief composites. The first was related to homophobia in fraternities (people in fraternities are homophobic, people in fraternities are accepting of homosexuality [reverse-scored], and fraternities do not accept homosexuality; Cronbach's $\alpha = .61$). The second involved relationships between alumni and current fraternity members (alumni of fraternities look back with nostalgia at their fraternity days, undergraduate fraternity members depend on alumni fraternity members for financial support, undergraduate fraternity members look up to alumni fraternity members, and undergraduate fraternity members respect alumni fraternity members; Cronbach's $\alpha = .70$). The third involved pledging and hazing (risk-free pledging creates less brotherhood, pledging into a fraternity is an important event, there are absolutely no benefits for fraternities that use pledge periods that involve physical and mental hazing [reverse-scored], pledging a fraternity is not an important event in the lives of fraternity members [reverse-scored]; Cronbach's $\alpha = .64$). The final composite addressed more general beliefs on the difficulty of being homosexual in the United States (being a homosexual in the U.S. can cause pain and turmoil; and in U.S. society, the life of a homosexual is trouble-free [reverse-scored]).

We also analyzed two single-item measures, "the use of condoms will not protect against AIDS (reverse-scored)" and "friendships between men are important."[3]

Although we did not include a no-story control group in the study reported here, previous research using this narrative showed significant differences between readers and nonreaders on the belief items "fraternities are homophobic," "friendships between men are important," "condoms protect against AIDS," "fraternities need alumni support," and "gay men are better off to hide their sexual orientation" (Garst, Green, Brock, & Chung, 2003). Undergraduate participants who had read the story showed more story-consistent beliefs than those who had not. Therefore, we have some confidence that the story can change beliefs about these topics.

---

[3]A second item related to condoms, "use of condoms during sex is very important," did not correlate with the AIDS item ($r = .05$, $p > .20$) and so was not included in the analysis.

Transportation scale.   The transportation scale (Green & Brock, 2000) contains 15 items assessing individuals' immersion into a narrative. It measures cognitive engagement, affective reactions, and the experience of mental imagery. The scale has shown good internal consistency, as well as discriminant and convergent validity. Participants answer each item on a scale of 1 (*not at all*) to 7 (*very much*). An example item is, "I was emotionally involved in the narrative while reading it." The scale score is computed by taking the mean of the individual items (Cronbach's $\alpha = .77$).

Perceived realism.   Participants completed a modified version of the Perceived Plausibility Subscale of the Perceived Reality Scale (Elliott, Rudd, & Good, 1983; see Appendix). Eight items judged to be most relevant to the narrative were used, including questions about the realism and believability of characters, setting, dialogue, and other aspects of the communication. An example item is, "People in this narrative are like people you or I might actually know." The scale score is computed by taking the mean of the individual items (Cronbach's $\alpha = .81$).

Manipulation check for reading instructions.   Participants were asked to recall the instructions they were given at the start of the study. They checked one of four options: relax and read it naturally, think carefully about whether the story matched my beliefs, no instructions were given, or don't remember.

Personal experience.   Participants were asked whether they had close friends or family who were homosexual (yes or no). Participants also reported their sexual orientation (heterosexual, homosexual, bisexual, or prefer not to say) and whether they were members of a fraternity or sorority. They also answered the question, "How familiar are you with the system of Greek life in American colleges?" on a 5-point scale ranging from 1 (*not familiar*) to 5 (*very familiar*).

Demographics.   Participants reported their age, race, and gender.

RESULTS

Hypothesis 1: Prereading Instruction Will Affect Transportation

All participants in the transportation and elaboration conditions correctly recalled their instructions. In the control condition, 15 participants did not remember the instructions, and 8 incorrectly chose either "relax" or "compare beliefs." However, the instruction set manipulations did not affect reported transportation, $F(2, 148) < 1, p > .20$ (*M* relaxation = 4.25, *M* elaboration = 4.36, *M* control = 4.40). Hypothesis 1 was not supported. Therefore, all subsequent analyses collapsed across instruction set conditions.

Hypothesis 2: Personal Experience Increases Transportation

Homosexual friend or family member.   As predicted by Hypothesis 2, personal experience was associated with transportation into the story. Specifically, individuals with close friends or family who were homosexual ($n = 73$) were more transported into the story than those who did not ($n = 79$), $F(1, 150) = 4.76, p < .05$ (M homosexual friends = 4.47, M no homosexual friends = 4.21).

Being homosexual might also have an impact on transportation into the narrative, but we did not have enough homosexual participants to provide an accurate test of this hypothesis. Of our sample, only 2 participants reported being homosexual, and 5 reported being bisexual. One person did not report sexual preference, and the remaining participants were heterosexual.[4]

Personal experience and transportation: Fraternities.   On average, individuals were moderately familiar with Greek life in American colleges ($M = 3.12$, $SD = 1.17$). Regression analysis revealed that greater knowledge predicted higher levels of transportation into the story ($\beta = .28, p < .01$). These results provided further support for Hypothesis 2.

Being a member of a fraternity or sorority might also have an impact on transportation into the narrative, but as with homosexuality, we had relatively low numbers of participants who reported such membership (14 fraternity members, 5 sorority members). Individuals who were members of fraternities or sororities did indeed show higher transportation, $F(1, 150) = 7.08, p < .01$ (M nonmembers = 4.27, M members = 4.74).

Hypothesis 3: Transportation Increases Perceived Realism

Overall, participants thought the story was realistic ($M = 5.41, SD = .84$). Transportation was positively correlated with perceived realism of the story ($r = .38, p < .05$). Individuals who were more transported thought that the events, settings, and characters were more believable. Thus, Hypothesis 3 was supported (although these results are based on measured transportation and thus do not allow us to determine the direction of causality).

---

[4]Homosexual or bisexual participants did report higher transportation into the story, but not significantly so, $F(1, 149) = 1.96, p > .10$ (M heterosexual = 4.31, M homosexual or bisexual = 4.70).

TABLE 1
Effect of Transportation on Beliefs

Belief Composite/Item	Transportation		
	β	t	p
Homophobia in fraternities	.23	2.87	.005
Alumni and current members	.27	3.44	.001
Pledging and hazing	.23	2.85	.005
Difficulty of homosexuality in the United States	.05	0.65	.520
Friendship between men	.28	3.51	.001
Condoms protect against AIDS	.17	2.08	.040

Hypothesis 4: Transportation Increases Endorsement of Story-Consistent Beliefs

As predicted, regression showed that transportation was positively associated with three of the four belief composites and with both single-item measures (see Table 1). Individuals who were more transported showed more story-consistent beliefs, except for the composite measure of the "difficulty of being homosexual in the United States." Thus, Hypothesis 4 was generally supported.

Hypothesis 5: Perceived Realism Mediates the Effect of Transportation on Beliefs

Regression analysis revealed that perceived realism was significantly related to only two of the beliefs: the homophobia in fraternities composite ($\beta = .24$, $p < .01$) and the alumni composite ($\beta = .16$, $p < .05$). For both composites, transportation remained a significant predictor of beliefs even when controlling for perceived realism. Therefore, contrary to Hypothesis 5, realism was not a plausible mediator of transportation effects for either measure (Baron & Kenny, 1986). This result suggested that, although transportation is related to realism, the effect of transportation on beliefs involves something beyond making the narrative world seem more real.

Supplemental Analyses

Individuals who have prior familiarity with story-relevant themes or issues may also be more likely to hold story-consistent beliefs. To rule out this potential artifact, we examined the relation between the familiarity measures and beliefs and the relation between transportation and beliefs controlling for familiarity.

Personal experience, transportation, and beliefs.   Having a homosexual friend or family member was not directly related to story-related beliefs, except for the difficulties of being a homosexual in the United States (the belief item that was not associated with transportation in our primary analyses). The effect of transportation on all other story-related beliefs remained significant even when controlling for whether the participant had friends or family who were homosexual. (See the top panel of Table 2.)

Greater knowledge about the Greek system was also not directly related to story-relevant beliefs, except for the pledging and hazing composite. However, the effect of transportation on the latter composite score remained marginally significant even when controlling for knowledge ($\beta = .15$, $p < .07$), suggesting that knowledge did not fully account for the effect of transportation on beliefs about pledging and hazing. The effect of transportation on all other story-related beliefs remained significant or marginally significant even when controlling for self-reported knowledge about the fraternity/sorority system. (See the bottom panel of Table 2.)

TABLE 2
Effect of Transportation on Beliefs Controlling for Previous Experience
(Homosexual Friend or Family Member) or Familiarity (Knowledge
About the Greek System)

Belief Composite/Item	Transportation			Homosexual Friend/Family		
	β	t	p	β	t	p
Homophobia in fraternities	.24	8.20	.004	−.01	−0.17	.860
Alumni and current members	.26	3.27	.001	.10	1.25	.120
Pledging and hazing	.24	7.43	.003	−.01	−0.19	.850
Difficulty of homosexuality in the United States	.02	0.28	.780	.24	3.01	.003
Friendship between men	.28	3.50	.001	.01	0.17	.870
Condoms do not protect against AIDS (R)	.19	2.32	.020	−.09	−1.06	.290

Belief Composite/Item	Transportation			Knowledge About Greek Life		
	β	t	p	β	t	p
Homophobia in fraternities	.23	2.73	.007	−.01	−0.11	.910
Alumni and current members	.24	2.90	.004	.11	1.35	.180
Pledging and hazing	.15	1.83	.070	.29	3.59	.001
Difficulty of homosexuality in the United States	.02	0.17	.860	.14	1.69	.090
Friendship between men	.29	3.46	.001	−.03	−0.39	.690
Condoms do not protect against AIDS (R)	.14	1.69	.090	.12	1.44	.160

Personal experience and perceived realism.   We were also interested in the direct effect of familiarity on perceptions of realism. Here, the pattern was mixed. Having a homosexual friend or family member did not influence judgments of story realism, $F(1, 150) = 1.34$, $p > .20$. However, knowledge about the fraternity system was a significant predictor of perceived realism ($\beta = .24$, $p < .01$); individuals who knew more about fraternities found the story to be more realistic.

Transportation and gender.   Men and women were equally transported into the story, $F(1, 149) < 1$, $p > .20$ (M men $= 4.34$, $SD = .71$; M women $= 4.33$, $SD = .77$). Gender also had no significant effect on realism or belief judgments, and so it was not considered in the previous analyses.

DISCUSSION

The study reported here supported our hypotheses that prior familiarity with story themes produces increased transportation (Hypothesis 2), that transportation is associated with greater perceptions of realism (Hypothesis 3), and that transportation is associated with endorsing more story-consistent beliefs (replicating prior research; Hypothesis 4). However, the study did not provide support for Hypothesis 1—that prereading instructions encouraging relaxation or elaboration could increase or decrease transportation, respectively. Hypothesis 5—that perceived realism would mediate the relationship between transportation and beliefs—was also not supported.

Manipulating Transportation

Prior knowledge led to an increase in transportation, but an attempt to manipulate transportation by changing readers' approach to the narrative (relaxing vs. elaborating) was not successful. Although other prereading instruction sets have been used in past research to change transportation levels (e.g., reducing transportation by having individuals focus on surface features of the text, such as grammar and difficulty level; see Green & Brock, 2000), these instructions did not appear to evoke differential experience of the narrative. Although the manipulation check showed that individuals remembered the instructions, unfortunately, we did not measure to what extent individuals tried to follow directions or to what extent they felt they were able to do so.

Perhaps readers were unable fully to follow the instructions (e.g., because it is hard to relax and read naturally in a laboratory setting). Also, our instructions did not provide specific techniques for how to achieve their stated objectives (relaxation or elaboration). Perhaps individuals need more detailed guidance (e.g., modeled on hypnosis instructions) concerning how to achieve transportation. It also is possible that instructions must be particularly powerful to override other effects on transportation, such as text quality or (as shown here) prior experience relevant to the story.

An approach that future research might take is to focus on a component (or specific components) of transportation. For example, imagery is one element of transportation, and readers might be instructed to form mental images of characters and settings. Another option would be to increase feelings for characters by using an empathy manipulation—that is, by instructing readers to put themselves in someone else's place or to take the perspective of another and imagine how that other feels in a given situation (e.g., Batson, Early, & Salvarani, 1997; Bourg, Risden, Thompson, & Davis, 1993). If these more specific instructions were successful, they might have the additional benefit of helping to clarify which components of transportation are responsible for belief change.

Familiarity and Transportation

This study highlighted one factor that apparently influences the extent to which individuals become transported into a narrative: their previous experience, or pre-existing tendencies to like or sympathize with a particular character. Specifically, individuals who had a friend or family member who shared a significant characteristic (in this case, sexual orientation) with the main character of the story were more likely to become transported into the narrative. This does not mean that it was impossible for individuals who did not have this relevant prior experience to become transported; people who were not close to homosexuals in real life did not show a transportation floor effect. They were still engaged in the narrative, but somewhat less strongly than their counterparts with relevant experience. However, these results do suggest that factors making it easier to identify with or understand a character can encourage transportation. Similar effects emerged with individuals who had more knowledge about the Greek system (or who were themselves members of fraternities or sororities).

Of interest, this knowledge or similarity produced higher transportation even though the view of homosexuality and fraternities presented in the narrative was not entirely positive. The story explored the difficulties of coming to terms with being homosexual and revealing this fact to others; in addition, negative aspects of fraternities were mentioned. Thus, transportation does not appear to be due simply to having a story reinforce positive views about known or liked groups.

Prior knowledge may influence transportation in several ways. Knowing a person similar to a character on a relevant dimension, or knowing about the character's situation, may make it easier to create mental images of characters or settings. This ease of imagining may also contribute to story enjoyment. Prior knowledge or similarity may also increase an individual's motivation to engage the story; the reader may feel that the story is more relevant to his or her life. As Tan (1996) noted, interest in a narrative is a self-enhancing process: A greater initial interest can lead to more cognitive and emotional engagement, which can make the narrative experience more rewarding. Finally, prior knowledge may encourage *remindings*—links between the story content and the reader's own life (Larsen & Laszlo, 1990; Schank & Abelson, 1995; Strange & Leung, 1999). These remindings may be an important means by which literature can enter life: Individuals generalize the particulars of story content and apply it to their own situations.

It is likely that not all prior knowledge, familiarity, or similarity is equal in creating increased transportation into a narrative. Indeed, superficial similarities may be less important than being able to relate to the basic conflicts, emotions, or situations experienced by the character. For example, in other research, we have asked participants to read a first-person diary-style narrative about a high school student's experimentation with drugs, including her euphoric first experiences with hallucinogens and the later negative consequences (a selection adapted from the novel *Go Ask Alice*, Anonymous, 1971). Manipulating whether the main character was the same gender as the participant did not affect transportation, nor did manipulating whether the main character attended the same school as the participant (Green, Butler, & Britt, 2003; Wheeler et al., 1999; but see Jose & Brewer, 1984, where a gender-matching manipulation increased liking among children). In the same study, however, there was a positive correlation between transportation and responses to an item asking whether "the experiences of the narrator are similar to ones that I have faced at some point." The recognition of identifiably shared experiences may be pivotal in the emergence of transportation.

One of the great benefits of literature is that it can allow individuals to walk in someone else's shoes, to experience situations, times, and cultures outside of one's own narrow slice of history and circumstance. Educators sometimes use stories to build empathy or increase understanding of others. The study reported here suggests that having some kind of similarity or link with a character can aid in this process. Furthermore, once individuals have become transported into the narrative, other lessons may then be learned.

Transportation and Perceived Realism

Results indicated that transportation and perceived realism were positively related; consistent with our hypotheses, individuals who were more transported thought that the story was more like real life. Although the study reported here cannot determine the direction of causality, transportation theory argues that immersion into a narrative world makes that narrative world seem more like a real place. In this study, transported readers thought that the situations were realistic and that the characters acted like real people would have acted.

Also, as predicted, transportation was positively associated with endorsement of beliefs implied by the narrative; individuals who were more immersed in the story also showed more story-consistent beliefs. This association was not an artifact of previous experience, however. The relationships between transportation and beliefs remained even when controlling for whether the participant had a homosexual friend or family member or the amount of knowledge participants had about fraternity life.

However, contrary to our expectations, in the study reported here, increased realism was not related to holding story-consistent beliefs. This finding may suggest that the perception of increased realism is not a primary pathway from transportation to endorsement of story-consistent beliefs. Perceived realism may be a side effect of transportation rather than the mechanism for affecting beliefs. Another possibility is that the perceived realism of the story was sufficiently high for all participants (e.g., above some psychological threshold of plausibility), and thus the increase in perceived realism between more and less transported readers was not sufficiently powerful to cause differential effects on beliefs. Indeed, the mean rating for plausibility was more than a point above the midpoint of the scale. Future work might use narratives that have a somewhat lower mean plausibility rating to provide more opportunity for any plausibility effects to emerge.

Future Directions

The study reported here did not address the role of reader choice in determining transportation and the way in which selection of literature may interact with familiarity or other factors. Participants in our study were assigned to read a particular narrative, whereas in many situations, readers can select a book from among their own favorite genres, authors, or topics. Readers may be especially drawn to texts where they have some pre-existing link with the characters. For example, television viewers are more likely to watch programs with content that matches their self-concept (Preston & Clair, 1994).

Further studies might also address the broader effects of narrative, particularly the extent to which reading a narrative affects attitudes toward social groups. Transportation into "Just as I Am" (Harris, 1996) did not appear to affect beliefs about the difficulty of being a homosexual in the United States, but we did not assess whether the narrative resulted in more positive feelings toward homosexual individuals. (Of course, this type of general attitude may be relatively strong and resistant to change from a single communication.) In addition, future research might explore the degree to which reading a transporting narrative influences overt behavior. For example, would individuals treat a homosexual fraternity member more kindly after reading the narrative?

Although some aspects of the transportation model of narrative persuasion (see Figure 1) have been empirically confirmed, others remain to be explored. Additional predictors of becoming transported into a narrative world, as well as further investigation of the mediators of transportation-based belief change, are promising areas for further inquiry.

ACKNOWLEDGMENTS

I thank Chris Chatham and Jeremy Yap for their assistance in running this study.

REFERENCES

Anonymous. (1971). *Go ask Alice*. Englewood Cliffs, NJ: Prentice-Hall.

Baron, R. M., & Kenny, D. A. (1986). The moderator–mediator variable distinction in social psychological research: Conceptual, strategic, and statistical considerations. *Journal of Personality and Social Psychology, 51*, 1173–1182.

Batson, D. C., Early, S., & Salvarani, G. (1997). Perspective taking: Imagining how another feels versus imagining how you would feel. *Personality and Social Psychology Bulletin, 23*, 751–758.

Bourg, T., Risden, K., Thompson, S., & Davis, E. C. (1993). The effects of an empathy-building strategy on 6th graders' causal inferencing in narrative text comprehension. *Poetics, 22*, 117–133.

Braun, I. K., & Cupchik, G. C. (2001). Phenomenological and quantitative analyses of absorption in literary passages. *Empirical Studies of the Arts, 19*(1), 85–109.

Bruner, J. S. (1986). *Actual minds, possible worlds*. Cambridge, MA: Harvard University Press.

Busselle, R. W., & Greenberg, B. S. (2000). The nature of television realism judgments: A reevaluation of their conceptualization and measurement. *Mass Communication and Society, 3*, 249–268.

Csikszentmihalyi, M. (1990). *Flow: The psychology of optimal experience*. New York: Harper & Row.

Elliott, W. R., Rudd, R., & Good, L. (1983, August). *Measuring the perceived reality of television: Perceived plausibility, perceived superficiality and the degree of personal utility*. Paper presented at the annual meeting of the Association for Education in Journalism and Mass Communication, Corvallis, OR.

Fazio, R. H., & Zanna, M. P. (1981). Direct experience and attitude-behavior consistency. In L. Berkowitz (Ed.), *Advances in experimental social psychology* (Vol. 14, pp. 161–202). New York: Academic.

Garst, J., Green, M. C., Brock, T. C., & Chung, S. (2003). *Fact versus fiction labeling of narrative and of speeches: Persuasion parity despite heightened scrutiny of fact*. Manuscript submitted for publication.

Gerrig, R. J. (1993). *Experiencing narrative worlds*. New Haven, CT: Yale University Press.

Green, M. C., & Brock, T. C. (2000). The role of transportation in the persuasiveness of public narratives. *Journal of Personality and Social Psychology, 79*, 701–721.

Green, M. C., & Brock, T. C. (2002). In the mind's eye: Transportation-imagery model of narrative persuasion. In M. C. Green, J. J. Strange, & T. C. Brock (Eds.), *Narrative impact: Social and cognitive foundations* (pp. 315–341). Mahwah, NJ: Lawrence Erlbaum Associates, Inc.

Green, M. C., Butler, D., & Britt, L. (2003). [Effect of character and reader similarity on transportation into narrative worlds]. Unpublished raw data.

Harris, E. L. (1996). Just as I am. In S. S. Ruff (Ed), *Go the way your blood beats : An anthology of lesbian and gay fiction by African-American writers* (pp. 487–498). New York: Holt.

Hoorn, J. F., Konijn, E. A., & Van der Veer, G. C. (2003). Virtual reality: Do not augment realism, augment relevance. *Upgrade—Human-Computer Interaction: Overcoming Barriers, 4*, 18–26.

Johnson, M. K., Hastroudi, S., & Lindsay, D. S. (1993). Source monitoring. *Psychological Bulletin, 114*, 3–28.

Jose, P. E., & Brewer, W. F. (1984). Development of story liking: Character identification, suspense, and outcome resolution. *Developmental Psychology, 20*, 911–924.

Larsen, S. F., & Laszlo, J. (1990). Cultural-historical knowledge and personal experience in appreciation of literature. *European Journal of Social Psychology, 20*, 425–440.

Miall, D. S., & Kuiken, D. (1994). Foregrounding, defamiliarization, and affect: Response to literary stories. *Poetics, 22*, 389–407.

Miall, D. S., & Kuiken, D. (2002). A feeling for fiction: Becoming what we behold. *Poetics, 30*, 221–241.

Nell, V. (1988). *Lost in a book: The psychology of reading for pleasure.* New Haven, CT: Yale University Press.

Oatley, K. (1999). Why fiction may be twice as true as fact: Fiction as cognitive and emotional simulation. *Review of General Psychology, 3*, 101–117.

Oatley, K. (2002). Emotions and the story worlds of fiction. In M. C. Green, J. J. Strange, & T. C. Brock (Eds.), *Narrative impact: Social and cognitive foundations* (pp. 39–69). Mahwah, NJ: Lawrence Erlbaum Associates, Inc.

Ottati, V., Rhoads, S., & Graesser, A. C. (1999). The effect of metaphor on processing style in a persuasion task: A motivational resonance model. *Journal of Personality and Social Psychology, 77*, 688–697.

Potter, W. J. (1988). Perceived reality in television effects research. *Journal of Broadcasting and Electronic Media, 32*, 23–41.

Prentice, D. A., & Gerrig, R. J. (1999). Exploring the boundary between fiction and reality. In S. Chaiken & Y. Trope (Eds.), *Dual-process theories in social psychology* (pp. 529–546). New York: Guilford.

Prentice, D. A., Gerrig, R. J., & Bailis, D. S. (1997). What readers bring to the processing of fictional texts. *Psychonomic Bulletin & Review, 5*, 416–420.

Preston, J. M., & Clair, S. A. (1994). Selective viewing: Cognition, personality, and television genres. *British Journal of Social Psychology, 33*, 273–288.

Schank, R. C., & Abelson, R. P. (1995). Knowledge and memory: The real story. In R. S. Wyer, Jr. (Ed.), *Advances in social cognition* (Vol. VIII, pp. 1–85). Hillsdale, NJ: Lawrence Erlbaum Associates, Inc.

Shapiro, M. A., & Chock, T. M. (2003). *Psychological processes in perceiving reality. Media Psychology, 5*(2), 163–198.

Slater, M. D. (1990). Processing social information in messages: Social group familiarity, fiction versus nonfiction, and subsequent beliefs. *Communication Research, 17*, 327–343.

Strange, J. J. (2002). How fictional tales wag real world beliefs: Models and mechanisms of narrative influence. In M. C. Green, J. J. Strange, & T. C. Brock (Eds.), *Narrative impact: Social and cognitive foundations* (pp. 315–341). Mahwah, NJ: Lawrence Erlbaum Associates, Inc.

Strange, J. J., & Leung, C. C. (1999). How anecdotal accounts in news and in fiction can influence judgments of a social problem's urgency, causes, and cures. *Personality and Social Psychology Bulletin, 25*, 436–449.

Tan, E. S. (1996). *Emotion and the structure of narrative film: Film as an emotion machine.* Mahwah, NJ: Lawrence Erlbaum Associates, Inc.

Tellegen, A. (1982). *Brief manual for the Differential Personality Questionnaire.* Unpublished manuscript, University of Minnesota, Minneapolis.

Vorderer, P., Knobloch, S., & Schramm, H. (2001). Does entertainment suffer from interactivity? The impact of watching an interactive TV movie on viewers' experience of entertainment. *Media Psychology, 3*, 343–363.

Wheeler, S. C., Green, M. C., & Brock, T. C. (1999). Fictional narratives change beliefs: Replications of Prentice, Gerrig, & Bailis (1997) with mixed corroboration. *Psychonomic Bulletin & Review, 6*, 136–141.

Zillmann, D. (1991). Empathy: Affect from bearing witness to the emotions of others. In J. Bryant & D. Zillmann (Eds.), *Responding to the screen: Reception and reaction processes* (pp. 135–167). Hillsdale, NJ: Lawrence Erlbaum Associates, Inc.

Zillmann, D. (1994). Mechanisms of emotional involvement with drama. *Poetics, 23*, 33–51.

APPENDIX
Perceived Realism Items (Adapted From Elliott et al., 1983)

- The dialogue in the narrative is realistic and believable.
- The setting for the narrative just doesn't seem real.
- People in this narrative are like people you or I might actually know.
- The way people really live their everyday lives is not portrayed very accurately in this narrative.
- Events that actually have happened or could happen are discussed in this narrative.
- This narrative shows that people have both good and bad sides.
- I have a hard time believing the people in this narrative are real because the basic situation is so far-fetched.
- This narrative deals with the kind of very difficult choices people in real life have to make.

DISCOURSE PROCESSES, *38*(2), 267–286

Locating Self-Modifying Feelings Within Literary Reading

Don Kuiken, Leah Phillips, Michelle Gregus, David S. Miall,
Mark Verbitsky, and Anna Tonkonogy
Department of Psychology
University of Alberta, Edmonton

Self-modifying feelings during literary reading were studied in relation to the personality trait, absorption. Participants read a short story, described their experience of 3 striking or evocative passages in the story, and completed the Tellegen Absorption Scale (Tellegen, 1982). Compared to readers with either low or moderate absorption scores, those high in absorption were more likely to report affective theme variations and self-perceptual shifts, especially during an emotionally complicated portion of the story. Further analyses indicated that, rather than emotional involvement per se, the relationship between absorption and self-perceptual shifts was mediated by the interaction between theme variations and a style of expressive reflection called metaphors of personal identification.

The enduring effects of literary texts on reader attitudes and beliefs have been attributed to both their narrative and stylistic aspects (cf. Hakemulder, 2000, for a review). Narrative features afford the greatest variety of influences: The complex situations, motives, and actions described in literary fiction may nurture the reader's empathic abilities; the presentation of convincingly developed characters may provide models the reader can emulate; the portrayed consequences of character actions may implicitly convey the cultural norms that shape the reader's activities; and the comparison of various characters' demeanor vis-à-vis a common dilemma may enrich the reader's reflection on the ethical principles that guide moral conduct. The stylistic features of literary texts arguably complement—and augment— the preceding effects of narrative: The style in which the narrative is presented may

Correspondence and requests for reprints should be sent to Don Kuiken, University of Alberta, Department of Psychology, P217 Biological Sciences Building, Edmonton, AB T6G 2E9 Canada. E-mail: dkuiken@ualberta.ca

defamiliarize and refresh the interpretation of conventionally conceived narrative elements, figurative forms may mark the narrator's evaluations of character actions and their consequences, and rhetorical devices may enhance the persuasive effects of the presented narrative.

Compared to the direct influences of narrative and stylistic features, the forms of reader "involvement" that enable or amplify the effects of literary reading are less well articulated. Beyond the cognitive strategies that constitute comprehension (e.g., concrete simulation of the narrative world), the most commonly proposed forms of reader involvement are transportation (Gerrig, 1993; Green & Brock, 2002), empathy (Halasz, 1996; Zillman, 1994), and identification (Holland, 1975). Each of these involves the reader's response to narrative features of the text (e.g., empathy with a character's feelings), rather than the reader's engagement with its stylistic features. Consequently, they collectively neglect a pivotal possibility: The stylistic aspects of a literary text may not only have direct effects (e.g., defamiliarization), but they also may initiate a form of reader reflexivity that is itself figurative. Readers may appropriate the text's figurative forms (e.g., by borrowing its metaphors) or transform its narrative elements into figurative forms (e.g., using a fictional battle as a metaphor) in reflective reference to aspects of their own lives.

Substantiation of this possibility would have two important implications. First, it would help to clarify how literary reading complicates and enlivens narrative presentations. Literary reading is that site in which the text and the reader's reflections (also understood as text) provide an intertextual blend of narrative and stylistic forms. Second, it would help to explain why reading-induced changes in attitudes and beliefs often remain compellingly evident to the reader, but resistant (e.g., as resistant as metaphors) to explicit articulation. Indeed, the effects of literary reading often are figuratively grasped as an altered sense of self that is not readily conveyed to others.

The study presented here contributes to the empirical substantiation of these possibilities (see also Kuiken, Miall, & Sikora, 2004). In what follows, we (a) distinguish two figurative forms of reader engagement with literary texts, (b) demonstrate that their recurrent form is characteristic of some readers' involvement in literary reading, and (c) provide evidence that individual differences in such involvement are predictive of the effects of literary reading on the reader's shifting sense of self.

THE FIGURATION OF SELF-MODIFYING FEELINGS

At times, readers of literary texts find themselves participating in an unconventional flow of feelings through which they realize something that they have not previously experienced—or at least that they have not experienced in the form provided by the text. When this occurs, the imagined world of the text can become unsettling. What is realized (recognized) also may become real-ized (made real) and carried forward as a changed understanding of the reader's own life-world. We propose that this process of real-ization through literary reading involves a form of reflexivity that is itself figurative. We also suggest that the feelings integral to such figurative real-ization be called *self-modifying feelings* to differentiate them from evaluative feelings toward the text as a whole; aesthetic feelings in response to stylistic variations; and narrative feelings in reaction to the setting, characters, and events (Miall & Kuiken, 2002).

Phenomenological studies (Kuiken & Miall, 2001; Sikora, Kuiken, & Miall, 1998) have identified a type of reading experience that is distinctively marked by self-modifying feelings. This type of reading, called *expressive enactment*, involves (a) the emergence of aesthetic feelings, as well as narrative feelings; (b) blurred boundaries between self and other, suggesting some kind of personal identification; and (c) iterative and figurative modification of an emergent affective theme. In the research presented here, we are especially concerned with how readers iteratively and figuratively modify an emergent affective theme. We suggest that such transformation of an emergent affective theme may be the locus not only of readers' changing understanding of the text, but also of their changing sense of themselves.

TWO FIGURATIVE FORMS OF SELF-IMPLICATION

Readers' sense of themselves becomes involved in literary reading through forms of engagement variously called identification or empathy. Despite considerable definitional diversity (Barnes & Thagard, 1997; Oatley & Gholamain, 1997; Zillman, 1994), these forms of self-implication generally involve the self-resonant understanding of another's experiential perspective—regardless of whether the other is a narrator, character, or personified object. The self-resonant understanding of such narrative elements is usually taken literally—as though it could not also be given a figurative form. In contrast, Cohen (1999) suggested that a reader's identification with a narrator, character, or personified object creates a self-implicating tension when the reader metaphorically enacts that figure's perspective. Comparison theories of metaphor, which suggest the transfer or mapping of one pre-established domain onto another, obscure this possibility. Interaction theories of metaphor, in contrast, attempt to explicate that generative tension, and Cohen invoked interaction theories of metaphor in his portrayal of identification in literary reading. When metaphors of personal identification displace the comparative grasp of resemblances between reader and other, there emerges, argued Cohen, a distinctive self-modifying tension.

In think-aloud studies of literary reading, metaphors of personal identification are concretely evident in some readers' comments. To appreciate this possibility, consider first the following example, taken from a study described more fully later in this paper, in which a reader, while reading a short story entitled "The Wrong House" by Katherine Mansfield (1945), engages the text in a manner that resembles simile rather than metaphor. Commenting on the author's description of a setting in which "the houses opposite looked as though they had been cut out with a pair of ugly steel scissors and pasted on to the grey paper sky" (Mansfield, 1945, p. 675), she says

> I could actually see the street and the houses. So there was great imagery there … it reminded me of the street that I lived on when I was young. We lived in a small town in southern Alberta … and the houses looked like that; they looked like they had been cut out with ugly steel scissors.

As this example affirms, the reflections evoked during reading often capture similarities between aspects of a personal memory and aspects of the world of the text. In this case, the comparison is explicit ("the houses looked like that"), which suggests that this reader's expression can be understood on the model of a simile (A is like B; my experience of the street in my home town is like the narrator's experience of the street in the story). As implied by the reader's simile, memory and story are symmetrical partners in an explicit comparison ("A is like B" is equivalent in meaning to "B is like A").

In contrast, consider the following example in which a different reader of "The Wrong House" (Mansfield, 1945) is commenting on the author's description of a moment in which the protagonist, the elderly Mrs. Bean, realizes that men attending a funeral coach are disembarking and approaching her door: "'No!,' she groaned. But yes, the blow fell, and for the moment it struck her down. She gasped, a great cold shiver went through her, and stayed in her hands and knees" (p. 676). This reader comments

> it just makes you realize that … your own mortality is something that can make you unable to think clearly … [W]hile you think you still are alive and well and able to take care of yourself and help others, somebody else has decided that you can't. And then [at times like this] you don't think that it's their problem, [but instead] that you somehow have been mistaken all this time and that it's time for you to give in and end everything, whether you're ready to or not … [A] passage like this makes you realize that some day, perhaps something like that will happen to you and scare the hell out of you because you know how close it could be for you.

This reader uses the pronoun *you* to speak inclusively, but still personally (e.g., "it just makes you realize"). While spelling out what Mrs. Bean is like in this scene (e.g., she was "unable to think clearly"; she realizes that "it's time … to give in"), this reader is also implicitly referring to herself as a person of the same kind. Although similarity is somehow at stake, this reader is not simply comparing Mrs. Bean and herself. Instead, as indicated by her choice of pronoun form, she identifies Mrs. Bean and herself as members of the same inclusive class. Comparison in this form is asymmetrical; that is, "A is B" is not equivalent in meaning to "B is A." To say, as this reader seems to do, that "I am Mrs. Bean" is not equivalent to saying that "Mrs. Bean is me." Such asymmetry suggests that, rather than comparison through simile, this reader is engaged in a metaphor of personal identification (Cohen, 1999).

The significance of metaphors of personal identification can be articulated according to Glucksberg and Keysar's (1990) interactive theory of metaphor. In that view, the reader's metaphoric identification of herself with Mrs. Bean creates an ad hoc class exemplified by Mrs. Bean, but also including herself. This metaphoric self-reference implicitly endows the reader with attributes of the ad hoc class exemplified by Mrs. Bean (e.g., those who are "unable to think clearly," who realize that "it's time … to give in," and so on) within constraints imposed by the reader's own self-understanding (e.g., that she is not old like Mrs. Bean). It also generates modifying feelings by prompting her to consider whether she possesses the previously unarticulated attributes of individuals in this class. Examination of the concluding passage in our reader's reflections substantiates this possibility: She is made to "realize" that "something like that will happen to [her] and scare the hell out of [her] because [she will] know how close it could be."

THE TEMPORALITY OF SELF-MODIFYING FEELINGS

The contrast between the preceding pair of commentaries suggests that self-implicating similes are less generative than metaphors of personal identification. The metaphoric form of self-implication creates an affinity between the reader and the text that simultaneously prompts openness to a different understanding not only of the text, but also of the reader herself. For this reason, it might be expected that the reader will say more about the theme that has been metaphorically identified. The originary metaphor of personal identification, in other words, may instigate additional attempts to clarify that self-implicating theme. Through subsequent modifications of this theme, readers may, in the words of Ingarden, attempt to "satiate [themselves] with the quality in question, to consolidate possession of it" (Ingarden, 1985, p. 114). A clear example of such an attempt is evident in the commentaries of the reader last quoted. Commenting on a passage in which Mrs.

Bean's maid pulls down the window blinds, apparently to protect Mrs. Bean from further distressing encounters with the outside world, she says

> Having somebody else pull down the blind in this story makes me feel like when other people make the decisions for you and take away your power over yourself, deciding when it's your time to be in darkness or to die, and when you have outlived your usefulness … A very uncomfortable feeling with the realization that someday I might get that way and other people are deciding things for me and feeling that I am really no longer really of usefulness and nothing but a silly old woman who has fallen asleep and gets jittery at the smallest things.

As in her response to the earlier passage, this reader uses the pronoun *you* to speak inclusively, but personally (e.g., "other people make the decisions for you and take away your power"). Through this inclusive expression, the reader again implicitly refers to herself as someone whose autonomy is placed in jeopardy as death approaches. In this variation on that theme, however, she emphasizes loss, rather than abdication, of this autonomy.

In this example and others that we have observed (Kuiken et al., 2004), variations on an emergent affective theme are experienced in a pulsing temporal pattern during literary reading. To use a musical analogy, this temporal pattern has the structure of a fugue in which a pivotal theme is progressively augmented or diminished, combined or contrasted, concretized or abstracted, and so on. The temporal dynamics of this fugal structure are seldom considered in discussions of identification, although, we suggest, they may be critical to understanding how literary reading enters the reader's life. One noteworthy exception is Iser (1978), who, although recognizing the reader's momentary identifications, also emphasized their "negation." "Invalidation" of one of the reader's identifications by another "situates the reader halfway between a 'no longer' and a 'not yet.'" Within that "blank," he argued, the possibility of changing the reader's sense of self emerges (Iser, 1978, p. 213). Iser, like Bakhtin (1981), suggested that identification with the perspective of a narrator, character, or personified object is best understood as one moment within a sequence of such dialogical, self-altering moments.

ABSORPTION AND SELF-MODIFYING READING

This theme-varying structure is not evident for all readers and, when evident, not uniformly present throughout the reading experience. The study presented here is an attempt to locate this theme-varying structure in relation to the personality trait absorption. Tellegen and Atkinson (1974; Tellegen, 1982) defined *absorption* as a disposition for having episodes of "total attention" that (a) fully engage one's representational resources, (b) heighten the sensed reality of the attentional object, and (c) alter experience of the attentional object and the self. Given its empirical association with openness to experience (McCrae & Costa, 1985; Radtke & Stam, 1991), especially with its aesthetic facets (Glisky, Tataryn, Tobias, Kihlstrom, & McConkey, 1991; Wild, Kuiken, & Schopflocher, 1995), we expected that absorption would predict self-modifying feelings and, hence, the fugal form of literary reading.

Absorption has been linked to several factors that plausibly mediate this form of literary reading. First, people who are high in absorption report visual–auditory synaesthesia (Rader & Tellegen, 1987) and vivid imagery (McConkey & Nogrady, 1986), including in response to visual art (Wild et al., 1995). These findings suggest that people high in absorption will also be responsive to the imaginal sources of figurative language. Second, people high in absorption report self-perceptual shifts during psychotherapy (Lloyd & Gannon, 1999) and intensive self-reflection (Kuiken, Carey, & Nielsen, 1987). These studies suggest that people high in absorption will be open to self-modifying feelings during literary reading. Third, people high in absorption report that the visual, musical, and literary arts influence their feelings in a way that is important in their everyday life (Wild et al., 1995). This finding is consistent with research indicating that people high in absorption describe themselves as motivated to read literary texts for insight (Miall & Kuiken, 1995).

In the study presented here, we examined the possibility that people high in absorption will report that, during literary reading, they re-express a theme and experience related shifts in self-perception.

METHOD

Participants

Fifty-eight introductory psychology students at the University of Alberta participated in this study for partial course credit. Forty-six were women (*M* age 21.08, range = 17–47), and 13 were men (*M* age 19.91, range = 17–30). A prerequisite to participation was that the participant's first language be English.

Procedures

Arriving at the laboratory in groups of three or four, participants first were given an overview of the study. They were told that (a) the study was concerned with how people respond to literature; (b) after reading a short story, they would be asked to identify and mark passages that they found striking or evocative; (c) they would then be asked to describe their thoughts and feelings about each marked passage;

(d) these comments on their thoughts and feelings would be tape-recorded; and (e) they would be asked to complete a personality questionnaire. They were also told that the information they provided would remain anonymous and confidential. On providing consent to participate, participants were guided to separate research rooms to ensure their privacy while they completed the research tasks.

To acquaint them with the procedures, participants were asked to read an excerpt from a short story entitled "The Trout" by Seán O'Faoláin (1980). After reading it at their own pace and as they normally would, they read it again to identify and mark any passages they found striking or evocative. In an adaptation of the self-probed retrospection technique (Larsen & Seilman, 1988), they then chose the one marked passage that they found most striking or evocative and, using a voice-activated tape recorder, described any "thoughts, feelings, images, or memories" that were part of their experience of that passage. Finally, they completed a nine-item Reading Experience Questionnaire (REQ) that assessed several aspects of their feelings and self-perceptions while reading that passage.

After the practice session, participants were asked to read a complete short story, "The Wrong House" by Katherine Mansfield (1945). They followed the same steps as for the practice story, except that they were asked to choose the three passages that they found most striking or evocative. Participants provided tape-recorded commentaries on their experience of each selected passage before completing the REQ for each of them. Finally, participants completed the Tellegen Absorption Scale (TAS; Tellegen, 1982) and were provided a complete debriefing.

Questionnaires

REQ. The REQ included 9 items assessing changes in feeling and self-perception while reading the marked passage. Each item was rated on a 5-point scale ranging from 1 (*not at all true*) to 5 (*extremely true*). One 3-item subscale, designed to assess feeling involvement, included items that asked about "feelings in reaction to situations or events in the story (e.g., feeling compassion for a character's frustration)," "resonance of my own feelings with those in the story (e.g., feeling in myself the mood of a setting)," and "an impression of the feelings that were expressed/embodied in the story" (Cronbach's $\alpha = .76$). Another 4-item scale, designed to reflect self-perceptual shifts, included items that asked about awareness of "feelings that I typically ignore," "feelings about myself (e.g., feelings of inferiority)," remembering "an event external to the story (e.g., an event that occurred in my personal life)," and anticipating "something that would happen in the future (e.g., something that might happen to me tomorrow)" (Cronbach's $\alpha = .53$).

TAS. The TAS (Tellegen, 1982) is a 34-item (true–false) measure consisting of items such as "The sound of a voice can be so fascinating to me that I can just go on listening to it"; "If I wish, I can imagine (or daydream) some things so vividly that they hold my attention as a good movie or story does"; and "Sometimes I experience things as if they were doubly real." Psychometric evaluation suggests that the scale is essentially unidimensional, with high inter-item consistency (Kuder-Richardson 20 = .86 in Wild et al., 1995; .81 in this sample) and high test–retest reliability (e.g., .92 in Tellegen, 1982). Roche and McConkey (1990) reviewed evidence that the TAS possesses construct validity as a measure of imaginative involvement. For the study presented here, we created a masked version of the TAS by administering it in a form that mixed its items with the 33 (true–false) items of the Crowne-Marlowe Social Desirability Scale (Crowne & Marlowe, 1964). The resulting 67-item questionnaire was presented to participants as a "series of statements a person might use to describe her or his attitudes, opinions, interests, and other characteristics."

Content Analyses

Three categories of response (affective theme variations, metaphors of personal identification, and similes of personal identification) were identified in participant commentaries on the passages they selected as especially striking or evocative. Two judges, blind to TAS scores and REQ ratings, scored each category of response, and disagreements were resolved in discussions involving both judges and the first author. Because these categories were created during close examination of commentaries from the study presented here, because their subtlety motivated frequent rereading and rescoring, and because precision in their use requires considerable experience, we did not calculate interjudge reliability estimates.

Affective theme variations. Affective theme variations were identified across the three commentaries. Theme variations occurred when, in response to either the second or third passages, the reader returned to an affective theme that had been described in comments on an earlier passage. We created a scale that reflected the following distinctions:

1. No repetition of a theme.
2. (Nonaffective) theme repetition without elaboration.
3. (Nonaffective) theme repetition with concrete situational elaboration.
4. Theme repetition with affective variation.
5. Theme repetition with affective variation and concrete situational elaboration.
6. Theme repetition with affective variation and feeling elaboration.

We then created a *composite measure of (peak) theme variations*, which was defined as the larger of the theme variation ratings for each reader's second and third commentaries.

In the following example (scored 6 on the preceding scale), the reader initially commented on Mrs. Bean's self-absorbed knitting, recalling her own turn toward that craft after accidental injury had severely restricted her activities:

> The first passage that struck me was of Mrs. Bean knitting. I began to knit shortly after, well not shortly after, about six months after being in a serious car accident. It was a change of lifestyle for me completely. I had gone from being extremely physical, training for body building competitions, to being completely sedentary. And a friend decided the best distraction for me was to learn to knit and crochet. Knitting, for me, began to be a time of productivity, where I was able to do nothing before a time of construction, a time that was warm because whatever I was knitting, as it increased in size, would be growing and becoming warm in my hands.

In her next commentary, in response to a narrative account of Mrs. Bean's shadowy sitting room, this reader reflected again on restricted activities. As before, she considered her inability to undertake or complete constructive projects (theme repetition), although the source of this frustrating inability was now the autumnal onset of long, dark nights (affective theme variation). Also, her feelings of frustration became more elaborately described (feeling elaboration): Through her account of the seasonal changes, she seemed metaphorically to revisit the time when, due to her accident, "life itself" was "closing in." In her words

> The second passage that really struck me was, "It seemed dusk already; dusk came floating into the room, heavy dark [sic], powdery dusk." That has been my experience as well late in the fall. It is not my favourite season of the year. Darkness comes way too early. It is a frustrating time because of commitments that have to be done … It just feels like life, not only the day time closing, but life itself is closing in on a person, that there isn't space to complete stuff that one had wanted to do, that things are becoming dark and cold, they're closing in on one. But more than that, that the opportunity to get things completed and finished is closing down on one before they are ready for it. And I think that's what was trying to be said in the story for poor Mrs. Bean as well.

Metaphors of personal identification.   *Metaphors of personal identification* were defined as commentaries in which the reader (a) made first-person reference to self and third-person reference to a story character; (b) occasionally used the pronoun *you* to indicate that some aspect of experience was shared by the reader, a story character, and others; and (c) used this pronoun form in conjunction with present tense verbs, suggesting that the shared experience was considered broad and enduring.

Example: It says that she had fallen into a cave whose walls were darkness. I guess it's the personal experience I've had ... After especially an event that shocks you, you don't always start thinking about it right away. Your mind just goes completely blank and you kind of don't believe it actually happened.

Similes of personal identification.

Similes of personal identification were defined as commentaries in which the reader (a) made first-person reference to self and third-person reference to a story character; (b) used explicitly comparative terms (e.g., "that was like ..."; "that reminded me of ...") to indicate recognition of personal experiences that were similar to the character's; and (c) portrayed these similarities as involving character traits, actions, motives, thoughts, attitudes, or feelings.

Example: ... when she talked about "two purl, two plain, woolinfront-oftheneedle," [that] reminded me of all the attempts that I've made to try and knit something ... So I very much kind of had images of myself at my grandmother's, of her teaching me how to knit at my own home in front of the TV set, knitting a red wool scarf for my brother.

A subset of these commentaries, which we have labeled *similes of empathic identification*, were similes of personal identification that explicitly portrayed similarities between the reader's and a character's attitudes or feelings. Other similarities might be acknowledged as well, but similarities in attitudes or feelings were at least mentioned.

Example: I feel like she feels. I have more goose bumps now. I can almost hear the footsteps of the horses fading away in the background. Scary: "the cave whose walls were darkness." I know that feeling well, not wanting to think of what happened 'cause it's scary.

RESULTS

Because individuals with high absorption scores sometimes differ systematically from those having either low or moderate scores (i.e., relations are not always linear), TAS scores (overall $M = 21.32$) were used to create groups with low (range = 8–19, $n = 17$), moderate (range = 20–23, $n = 24$), and high (range = 24–33, $n = 17$) absorption scores.

Primary Analyses

Theme variations.   A one-way analysis of variance (ANOVA) assessing the relation between absorption and (peak) theme variations was statistically significant, $F(2, 56) = 3.781$, $MSE = 2.913$, $p < .029$. Planned contrasts indicated that the average theme variation rating for high-absorption participants was greater than the average theme variation rating for those with low ($p < .032$) or moderate ($p < .017$) absorption scores (see Table 1). Thus, as expected, in response to the second and third marked passages, readers with high absorption scores were more likely to report modification of previously expressed affective themes.

Self-perceptual shifts.   One-way ANOVAs assessing the relation between absorption and the REQ self-perceptual shifts scale indicated that, on the second (but neither the first nor third) marked passage, the relation between absorption and self-perceptual shift ratings was statistically significant, $F(2, 55) = 3.806$, $MSE = 0.621$, $p < .028$. Planned contrasts indicated that the average self-perceptual shift rating for high-absorption participants was greater than the average self-perceptual shift rating for those with low ($p < .010$) or moderate ($p < .035$) absorption scores (see Table 1). Thus, while reading the middle portion of the story, which depicted the encounter between Mrs. Bean and the men from the funeral coach, high-absorption readers were more likely to report a shifting sense of self.

Together, these findings are consistent with the expectation that absorption would be associated with affective theme variations and with a shifting sense of self during reading—even though the latter relationship was specific to the middle portion of the story. However, we unexpectedly found that (peak) theme variation ratings were uncorrelated with reported shifts in self-perception in response to either the second passage or the other two passages (all p values > .14). So, we could not confidently conclude that theme variations mediated that self-perceptual outcome.

TABLE 1
Mean (Peak) Theme Variation and Self-Perceptual Shift Scores
as a Function of Absorption

Dependent Measures	Absorption Score		
	Low	Moderate	High
(Peak) theme variation ratings	2.33	2.38	3.71*
Self-perceptual shifts for Passage 1	2.24	2.45	2.26
Self-perceptual shifts for Passage 2	2.02	2.18	2.72*
Self-perceptual shifts for Passage 3	2.23	2.46	2.32

*Means differ significantly from low and moderate absorption groups at $p < .05$.

Supplemental Analyses

Theme variations and metaphors of personal identification.   Our original expectation was that metaphors of personal identification would generate affective theme variations and that such exploratory reflection within a series of theme variations would lead to self-perceptual shifts. However, that model is inconsistent with the finding that theme variations did not predict self-perceptual shifts. As an alternate model, we considered whether theme variations might lead to such shifts only when the generative force of metaphors of personal identification persists as part of their structure. So, we examined the possibility that the relationship between absorption and self-perceptual shifts is mediated by the interaction between metaphors of personal identification and theme variations. First, we conducted a two-way ANOVA with (a) the presence or absence of metaphors of personal identification as a categorical between-subjects variable, (b) (peak) theme variation ratings as a continuous between-subjects variable, and (c) TAS absorption scores as the dependent variable. Only the interaction between metaphors of personal identification and theme variations was significant, $F(1, 53) = 5.157$, $MSE = 30.06$, $p < .027$. Among readers who engaged the text using metaphors of personal identification, theme variations were associated with higher absorption scores ($r = .647, p < .007$); for those who did not use metaphors of personal identification, the relationship between theme variations and absorption was negligible ($r = .085, ns$).

Second, we conducted an analogous two-way ANOVA with self-perceptual shifts in response to the second passage as the dependent variable. Again, there was a significant interaction between metaphors of personal identification and theme variations, $F(1, 52) = 4.094, MSE = 0.619, p < .048$. When readers engaged the text using metaphors of personal identification, theme variations tended to be positively correlated with reported self-perceptual shifts in response to the second passage ($r = .465, p < .070$); when readers did not use metaphors of personal identification, theme variations were, if anything, negatively correlated with these self-perceptual shifts ($r = -.158, ns$).

Furthermore, when absorption was added to the preceding ANOVA as a covariate, the effect of the interaction between metaphors of personal identification and theme variations became negligible: Partial eta squared declined from .073 to .002. This decline is consistent with a model in which the relationship between absorption and self-perceptual shifts, particularly in response to the second marked passage, is mediated by the interaction between metaphors of personal identification and theme variations (Baron & Kenny, 1986). In other words, among readers who are high in absorption, engaging the text by extending their metaphors of personal identification across theme variations initiates self-perceptual shifts.

Other potential mediators of self-perceptual shifts.   The preceding pattern of relationships is specific to metaphors of personal identification. Although metaphors of personal identification are plausibly associated with feeling involvement, participants reporting metaphors of personal identification actually did not report greater feeling involvement on the REQ ($r = -.079$, *ns*). Moreover, two-way ANOVAs indicated that neither feeling involvement, nor theme variations, nor their interaction predicted absorption scores or self-perceptual shifts. Similarly, metaphors of personal identification plausibly occur within the context of similes of personal identification (perhaps especially within the context of similes of empathic identification). That expectation is warranted: Readers providing metaphors of personal identification were more likely to provide similes of personal identification ($r = .297, p < .024$), especially similes of empathic identification ($r = .390, p < .002$). However, two-way ANOVAs indicated that neither similes of personal identification, nor theme variations, nor their interaction predicted absorption scores or self-perceptual shifts. And, two-way ANOVAs indicted that neither similes of empathic identification, nor theme variations, nor their interaction predicted absorption scores or self-perceptual shifts. In none of the preceding analyses, then, was the pattern for feeling involvement, similes of personal identification, or similes of empathic identification comparable to the pattern observed for metaphors of personal identification. Metaphors of personal identification, but neither feeling involvement, nor similes of personal identification, nor similes of empathic identification, interacted with theme variations to mediate the effects of absorption on self-perceptual shifts during reading.

Absorption and feeling involvement.   In general, there was no relation between absorption and feeling involvement. One-way ANOVAs with absorption as the independent variable and REQ feeling involvement scores for the three marked passages as dependent variables indicated no reliable differences. However, responses to an REQ item asking whether readers' experience of the marked passage involved feelings about themselves (rather than about the story) did vary as a function of absorption, $F(2, 55) = 6.888$, $MSE = 1.351$, $p < .002$. Specifically in response to the second marked passage, the average rating for self-directed feelings among high-absorption participants (3.06) was greater than the average rating for self-directed feelings among those with low ($1.71, p < .001$) or moderate ($1.92, p < .003$) absorption scores. The middle section of the story, during which high-absorption readers also were more likely to report self-perceptual shifts, also evoked self-directed feelings in those readers.

Selected passages.   We examined the passages that participants marked as striking or evocative to determine whether there was any consistency in their selections. There was some consistency in the first two selections, but not the third. The modal first choice (selected by 18 of the 58 participants) was a highly foregrounded passage describing the opening scene in which we find Mrs. Bean rhythmically and routinely knitting clothing for charity:

> She sat at the dining-room window facing the street. It was a bitter autumn day; the wind ran in the street like a thin dog; the houses opposite looked as though they had been cut out with a pair of ugly steel scissors and pasted on to the grey paper sky. (Mansfield, 1945, p. 675)

The modal second choice (selected by 15 participants) was a passage in which Mrs. Bean is shocked to see a funeral coach attendant approaching her door:

> What was this? What was happening? What could it mean? Help, God! Her old heart leaped like a fish and then fell as the glass coach drew up outside her door, as the outside men scrambled down from the front, swung off the back, and the tallest of them, with a glance of surprise at the windows, came quickly, stealthily, up the garden path. (Mansfield, 1945, p. 676)

Twelve other passages selected for the second commentary immediately followed this one. Collectively, these passages describe Mrs. Bean's dismay as the funeral attendant approaches her door, her flustered distress as he realizes that he has gone to the "wrong 'ouse," and her ensuing and secretly unsettled disorientation "as if she had fallen into a cave whose walls were darkness" (Mansfield, 1945, p. 677). There was no evidence that absorption affected the likelihood that any particular passage would be selected as striking or evocative.

DISCUSSION

The results of this study help to locate self-modifying feelings within literary reading. Readers who engaged a literary text through variations in an affective theme were more likely to be high in absorption. Also, readers who reported shifts in self-perception, especially in response to emotionally complicated passages in a text, were more likely to be high in absorption. However, our findings are not compatible with a model according to which the effect of absorption on self-perceptual shifts is mediated simply by reader theme variations. Instead, they indicate that the interaction between theme variations and metaphors of personal identification mediate these effects. Affective theme variations only lead to self-perceptual shifts when metaphors of personal identification persist as part of their structure. High-absorption readers, who showed such persistence more regularly than did low-absorption readers, also more regularly reported shifts in self-perception. In sum, high-absorption readers report self-modifying feelings during reading because they re-express affective themes within that form of self-implicating reflection called metaphors of personal identification.

This model specifically implicates metaphors of personal identification. Theme variations within the context of similes of personal identification were not associated with the same self-perceptual outcome—even when they involved empathic reference to similarities between the reader's and the story character's attitudes or feelings. The specificity of these relationships affirms the self-modifying force attributed to metaphors of personal identification in Cohen's (1999) and our account. Theme variations within the context of metaphors of personal identification prompt readers to consider iteratively whether they possess the attributes of individuals in the ad hoc class exemplified by a selected story character. Such freshly articulated self-perceptual possibilities depend on the generativity that is posited by interaction theories of metaphor; they do not arise through the simile-like structure of many readers' experience of literary texts.

Procedures used in the study presented here indicate that metaphors of personal identification can be effectively discerned in readers' comments on their reading experience. The structured combination of self-reference (I), inclusive pronominal reference to self and others (you), and present-tense verbs identifies a mode of engagement that can be meaningfully differentiated from other forms of self-implication in reader commentaries. Similarly, we have found that variations on an affective theme can be systematically differentiated from repetitions of situationally contextualized attributions. Nonetheless, despite productive use of these content analytic categories in the study presented here, more should be done to articulate concretely these discriminations.

Also, the moderate level of internal consistency in the measure of self-perceptual shifts used in this study suggests the need for psychometric refinement. Despite evidence of its factorial and construct validity in situations that involve intensive self-reflection (Kuiken et al., 1987; Kuiken & Nielsen, 1996), more precise measures of the shifts in self-perception that occur during reading are required. In particular, we need to develop additional items to reflect emerging awareness of feelings that are typically ignored, uncommon reminiscences evoked by passages in the text, and the anticipation of novel forms of future conduct.

Despite these limitations, the study presented here provides useful information about when and for whom literary reading adds intricacy to reflection on the forms of life in which the reader participates. The theme variations articulated here are somewhat reminiscent of the alternating identifications through which, according to Carroll (2002), readers refine concepts of virtue and the conditions of their application. However, it is important to contrast our characterization of theme variations with the perspectival transitions that occur when a reader identifies first with one character's perspective and then another's. It is also important to contrast our characterization with the perspectival transitions that occur as a reader becomes acquainted with a character through a sequence of contrasting narrative events.

The theme variations that readers reported in our study include these, but also perspectival transitions afforded by shifts in figurative style. We have begun to examine how these perspectival transitions are marked by the reader's own fluctuations in expressive style (e.g., through metaphorical or allegorical interpretive reflection; Sikora et al., 1998). Examination of theme variations in this way begins to touch closely on the criteria by which we identify metaphors of personal identification. Is the movement from explicitly comparative, simile-like expressions to metaphors of personal identification already a type of theme variation? Considerations such as these may help us understand the statistical interaction, observed in the study presented here, between metaphors of personal identification and theme variations in the prediction of self-perceptual shifts during reading.

They may also help us understand why readers who are high in absorption are predisposed to re-express affective themes through metaphors of personal identification. The self-altering aspect of Tellegen and Atkinson's (1974) conception of absorption is not very well understood. There is evidence, including results from the study presented here, that the imaginative involvement associated with absorption is more than simple emotional involvement. We found that absorption did not predict REQ ratings of feeling involvement, and similar findings are common in the literature (cf. Foster, Webster, & Smith, 1997). But neither is the imaginative involvement associated with absorption simply reducible to imagery vividness—even though that aspect of the life of imagination is more consistently predicted by the TAS (cf. Roche & McConkey, 1990). Instead, we suggest, under certain conditions, such as are afforded by literary reading, absorption predisposes people to experience self-modifying feelings within imaginal activity. This self-altering aspect of absorption, which helps to locate it within the "openness to experience" domain in personality research, may be especially important to clarify.

Because the results of absorption research have been most fruitful when person–situation interactions are considered, absorption per se is not a satisfactory—and certainly not a complete—explanation for the self-perceptual shifts prompted by literary reading. The study of absorption within systematically varied reading conditions may usefully supplement this attempt to locate self-modifying feelings in literary reading. For example, Tellegen (1981) suggested that high-absorption people adopt an experiential orientation toward imaginal activity, whereas low-absorption people tend to adopt an instrumental orientation. If so, manipulations that undermine instrumentality during literary reading, as proposed by aesthetic attitude theory (Fenner, 1994), may prompt low- or moderate-absorption readers to engage the text not only affectively (Wild & Kuiken, 1992), but also through theme-varying metaphors of personal identification. Under these circumstances, readers more generally may enter the world of the text and emerge with a changed sense of themselves.

It will be important to locate this subtly changed sense of self among the array of attitudes and beliefs usually examined in research on the effects of literary reading. Reading-induced change in one's sense of self may accompany, or even mediate, the other purported effects of literary reading, such as the enhancement of empathic abilities, the enrichment of reflection on moral issues, and so on. It will also be important to determine whether reading-induced changes in one's sense of self are more likely to occur in response to literary than to nonliterary narratives. Whether there are not only distinctively literary reading experiences, but also distinctive effects of literary reading, is a question that can be freshly considered in light of these findings.

ACKNOWLEDGMENTS

Portions of this article were presented at the Conference of the International Society for the Empirical Study of Literature (IGEL), in Pécs, Hungary, August 21–24, 2002. The research reported here was supported by a grant from the Social Sciences and Humanities Research Council of Canada.

REFERENCES

Bakhtin, M. M. (1981). *The dialogic imagination: Four essays* (C. Emerson & M. Holquist, Trans.). Austin: University of Texas Press. (Original work published 1978)

Barnes, A., & Thagard, P. (1997). Empathy and analogy. *Dialogue: Canadian Philosophical Review, 36*, 705–720.

Baron, R. M., & Kenny, D. A. (1986). The moderator-mediator variable distinction in social psychological research: Conceptual, strategic, and statistical considerations. *Journal of Personality and Social Psychology, 51*, 1173–1182.

Carroll, N. (2002). The wheel of virtue: Art, literature, and moral knowledge. *Journal of Aesthetics & Art Criticism, 60*, 3–26.

Cohen, T. (1999). Identifying with metaphor: Metaphors of personal identification. *Journal of Aesthetics and Art Criticism, 57*, 399–409.

Crowne, D. P., & Marlowe, D. (1964). *The approval motive: Studies in evaluative dependence.* New York: Wiley.

Fenner, D. E. W. (1994). *The aesthetic attitude.* Atlantic Highlands, NJ: Humanities Press.

Foster, P. S., Webster, D. G., & Smith, E. W. L. (1997). The psychophysiological differentiation of emotional memories. *Imagination, Cognition and Personality, 17*, 111–122.

Gerrig, R. J. (1993). *Experiencing narrative worlds.* New Haven, CT: Yale University Press.

Glisky, M. L., Tataryn, D. J., Tobias, B. A., Kihlstrom, J. F., & McConkey, K. M. (1991). Absorption, openness to experience, and hypnotizability. *Journal of Personality and Social Psychology, 60*, 263–272.

Glucksberg, S., & Keysar, B. (1990). Understanding metaphorical comparisons: Beyond similarity. *Psychological Review, 97*, 3–18.

Green, M. C., & Brock, T. C. (2002). In the mind's eye: Transportation-imagery model of narrative persuasion. In M. C. Green, J. J. Strange, & T. C. Brock (Eds.), *Narrative impact: Social and cognitive foundations* (pp. 315–341). Mahwah, NJ: Lawrence Erlbaum Associates, Inc.

Hakemulder, J. (2000). *The moral laboratory: Experiments examining the effects of reading literature on social perception and moral self-knowledge.* Amsterdam: Benjamins.

Halasz, L. (1996). General and personal meaning in literary reading. In R. J. Kreuz & M. S. MacNealy (Eds.), *Empirical approaches to literature and aesthetics: Advances in discourse processes* (Vol. 52, pp. 379–396). Norwood, NJ: Ablex.

Holland, N. N. (1975). *Five readers reading.* New Haven, CT: Yale University Press.

Ingarden, R. (1985). Aesthetic experience and aesthetic object. In P. J. McCormick (Ed.), *Selected papers in aesthetics* (pp. 107–132). Washington, DC: Catholic University Press.

Iser, W. (1978). *The act of reading: A theory of aesthetic response.* Baltimore: Johns Hopkins University Press.

Kuiken, D., Carey, R., & Nielsen, T. (1987). Moments of affective insight: Their phenomenology and relations to selected individual differences. *Imagination, Cognition and Personality, 6,* 341–364.

Kuiken, D., & Miall, D. S. (2001). Numerically aided phenomenology: Procedures for investigating categories of experience. *Forum Qualitative Sozialforschung/Forum: Qualitative Social Research, 2*(1). Retrieved May 25, 2004, from http://qualitative-research.net/fqs/fqs-eng.htm

Kuiken, D., Miall, D. S., & Sikora, S. (2004). Forms of self-implication in literary reading. *Poetics Today, 25*(2), 171–203.

Kuiken, D., & Nielsen, T. A. (1996). Individual differences in orienting activity mediate feeling realization in dreams: I. Evidence from retrospective reports of movement inhibition. *Dreaming, 6,* 201–217.

Larsen, S. F., & Seilman, U. (1988). Personal remindings while reading literature. *Text, 8,* 411–429.

Lloyd, B. F., & Gannon, P. M. (1999). Personality as a predictor of treatment experiences: A combined focus on relaxation and catharsis. *Imagination, Cognition, and Personality, 19,* 39–58.

Mansfield, K. (1945). The wrong house. In *Collected stories of Katherine Mansfield* (pp. 675–678). London: Constable.

McConkey, K. M., & Nogrady, H. (1986). Visual Elaboration Scale: Analysis of individual and group versions. *Journal of Mental Imagery, 10,* 37–46.

McCrae, R. R., & Costa, P. T. (1985). Openness to experience. In R. Hogan & W. H. Jones (Eds.), *Perspectives in personality* (Vol. 1, pp. 145–172). Greenwich, CT: JAI.

Miall, D. S., & Kuiken, D. (1995). Aspects of literary response: A new questionnaire. *Research in the Teaching of English, 29,* 37–58.

Miall, D. S., & Kuiken, D. (2002). A feeling for reading: Becoming what we behold. *Poetics, 30,* 221–241.

Oatley, K., & Gholamain, M. (1997). Emotions and identification. In M. Hjort & S. Laver (Eds.), *Emotion and the arts* (pp. 263–281). New York: Oxford University Press.

O'Faoláin, S. (1980). The trout. In *Collected stories of Seán O'Faoláin* (Vol. 1, pp. 383–386). London: Constable.

Rader, C. M., & Tellegen, A. (1987). An investigation of synaesthesia. *Journal of Personality and Social Psychology, 52,* 981–987.

Radtke, H., & Stam, H. J. (1991). The relationship between imaginal ability and hypnotic sensibility: Context effects re-examined. *International Journal of Clinical and Experimental Hypnosis, 39,* 39–56.

Roche, S., & McConkey, K. (1990). Absorption: Nature, assessment, and correlates. *Journal of Personality and Social Psychology, 59,* 91–101.

Sikora, S., Kuiken, D., & Miall, D. S. (1998, August). *Enactment versus interpretation: A phenomenological study of readers' responses to Coleridge's "The Rime of the Ancient Mariner."* Paper presented at the conference of the International Society for the Empirical Study of Literature, Utrecht, The Netherlands.

Tellegen, A. (1981). Practicing the two disciplines for relaxation and enlightenment: Comment on "Role of the feedback signal in electromyograph biofeedback: The relevance of attention" by Qualls and Sheehan. *Journal of Experimental Psychology: General, 110,* 217–226.

Tellegen, A. (1982). *Brief manual for the Multidimensional Personality Questionnaire.* Unpublished manuscript, Department of Psychology, University of Minnesota, Minneapolis.

Tellegen, A., & Atkinson, G. (1974). Openness to absorbing and self-altering experiences ("absorption"), a trait related to hypnotic susceptibility. *Journal of Abnormal Psychology, 83,* 268–277.

Wild, T. C., & Kuiken, D. (1992). Aesthetic attitude and variations in reported experiences of a painting. *Empirical Studies of the Arts, 10,* 57–78.

Wild, T. C., Kuiken, D., & Schopflocher, D. (1995). The role of absorption in experiential involvement. *Journal of Personality and Social Psychology, 69,* 569–579.

Zillman, D. (1994). Mechanisms of emotional involvement with drama. *Poetics, 23,* 33–51.